USED
BOOK

8/2/15

USED
PRICE

Sell USED
Buy USED

AT THE MSU
BOOK STORE

$ 970

D1557330

FORMATIVE YEARS IN BUSINESS

A Long-Term AT&T Study of Managerial Lives

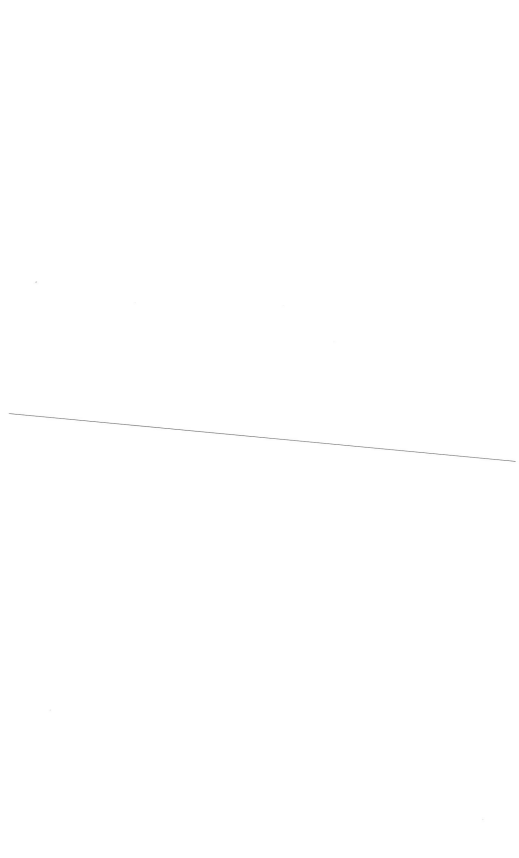

FORMATIVE YEARS IN BUSINESS

A Long-Term AT&T Study of Managerial Lives

DOUGLAS W. BRAY
RICHARD J. CAMPBELL
DONALD L. GRANT

American Telephone and Telegraph Company

A Wiley-Interscience Publication

JOHN WILEY & SONS, New York • London • Sydney • Toronto

Copyright © 1974, by John Wiley & Sons, Inc.

All rights reserved. Published simultaneously in Canada.

No part of this book may be reproduced by any means, nor transmitted, nor translated into a machine language without the written permission of the publisher.

Library of Congress Cataloging in Publication Data:

Bray, Douglas Weston.
Formative years in business: a long-term
AT&T study of managerial lives.

"A Wiley-Interscience publication."
Bibliography: p.
1. Executives—Case studies.   2. Executives—
Recruiting.   3. Psychology, Industrial.
4. Personality.   I. Campbell, Richard J., joint
author.   II. Grant, Donald L., joint author.
III. Title.

HF5500.2.B7   658.4'07'111   73-15990
ISBN 0-471-09810-8

Printed in the United States of America

10 9 8 7 6 5 4 3 2

To

ROBERT K. GREENLEAF

PREFACE

This book is the first major report drawn from the data of the Management Progress Study. The Study is an ambitious piece of longitudinal research on the life of managers in one large business, the Bell System.

Formative Years in Business is by no means a complete or final report of the Study. It includes only those subjects who became managers by being taken on as "college recruits." It covers only the first eight years of a continuous Study now in its eighteenth year. Perhaps most important, this report represents only a first pass at the voluminous Study materials. It describes the scope of the global findings.

This book is not written for professional researchers or technicians although the authors hope they will find much of interest in it. Our intent has been to communicate straightforwardly and concisely to those responsible for management selection and development within organizations, to those who educate and advise young people destined for managerial careers, and to managers themselves. In order to keep the text as uncluttered as possible statistical data not directly related to the presentation have been placed in the Appendix.

Further exploration of the Study data is continuing and will be reported in technical articles and, hopefully, additional volumes. A companion volume clearly called for is one covering the remainder of our subjects, those who reached management not as college recruits but by working their way up from the ranks. Other studies, now underway, will apply Management Progress Study methods to management hires of the 1970's. These studies will include substantial numbers of minority groups and women not represented in the 1956-60 sample.

Many people, over 100, have made important contributions to carrying out this Study. Some helped assess the recruits, others conducted the personal interviews, still others interviewed managers who knew or supervised the recruits. All deserve much gratitude. Our special thanks go to Walter Katkovsky and Joseph F. Rychlak, who contributed a chapter each to this book in addition to being involved in many phases of the Study since its inception; to Warren D. Bachelis who served many times as an assessor and whose rapport with our subjects through many years of follow-up interviewing was (and is) of great importance; to Albertus Derks, whose knowledge of the Bell System was invaluable in his many comprehensive interviews with the supervisors of the recruits; to John Hemphill, who made major contributions to the assessment center exercises; and to Robert C. Benfari, H. Weston Clarke, Jr., C. Keith Conners, William S. Felton, John Paul McKinney, Murray S. Plissner, and Donald L. Robinson.

We must also express admiration for the executives of the American Telephone & Telegraph Company who have supported the continuation of the Management Progress Study for so many years. As far as the authors are aware, there has never been a serious threat to the Study, even in lean, budget-cutting periods. No attempt has ever been made to breach the confidentiality of the individual records.

Finally, our greatest thanks must go to the subjects of the Study. They have twice participated in three-day assessment centers, and for some years they have agreed to annual interviews of great length. Most of them have answered every question we cared to ask. Even those who have not worked for the Bell System for a decade are still very much with the Study. No subject has received any tangible recompense for his efforts, not even a report on his own career.

We feel that our own efforts are inadequate to compensate for the contributions of so many, but we hope that all those who have worked on, supported, or participated in the Study will consider *Formative Years in Business* at least a first payment.

DOUGLAS W. BRAY
RICHARD J. CAMPBELL
DONALD L. GRANT

New York, New York
September 1973

CONTENTS

TABLES

FIGURES

FORMATIVE YEARS IN BUSINESS

A Long-Term AT&T Study of
Managerial Lives

1

THE MANAGEMENT
PROGRESS STUDY

Students of human behavior have mapped the earlier years of life with painstaking thoroughness. We know the exact age, in weeks, at which the average infant will be able to pick up a cube by opposing his thumb and forefinger, and we know the importance for later personality development of parental behavior during the child's early years. The processes by which children learn in school have been the subject of countless experiments.

We know much, therefore, about the preparatory period of life, but when the individual emerges from the high school or college into what we might call the performance period, we quickly run out of knowledge. Psychologist Robert W. White lamented this circumstance some years ago in his memorable *Lives in Progress* (White, 1952):

> Much as we know about personality, there is a serious gap at the very center of the subject. Individual lives moving forward amid natural circumstances have received almost no scientific study and have played almost no part in our current understanding.

1

One might wonder that the preparatory institutions, the schools and colleges, manifest so little curiosity about the later lives of their products. They are concerned to some degree with whether their graduates find appropriate employment, it is true; but how successful the graduates are, whether they are happy or alienated, what they are contributing to society, whether their intellectual growth continues—these questions are not vigorously pursued.

Perhaps the difficulties in following graduates into adult life are partly to blame. Not only do the young people disperse geographically, but they fan out into all manner of careers. It is no small job to track them continuously or even to find them all a few years after graduation. In addition, what criteria are to be used? What is success? How do you measure happiness? How do you rank contributions to society? Even if some agreement could be reached on these issues, securing hard data would require considerable cooperation on the part of the graduate, and often such cooperation would be difficult to obtain. These are some of the obstacles that underlie, although they do not excuse, the dearth of longitudinal studies of young people after they leave school.

UTILIZATION OR DEVELOPMENT?

Society seems to make an abrupt shift in its stance toward the individual once he enters the world of work. In school the emphasis has been on development; now it is on utilization. We try to guide people into the careers for which they are best suited, and the employers—whether they be private industry, government, or the schools and universities themselves—select, classify, and assign people to match them as they are to particular jobs. It is assumed, of course, that some will move ahead out of their first assignments to more demanding and rewarding positions because of the ability and motivation they *already* possess. The emphasis is on letting people find their level rather than on further development.

This passive utilization approach is characteristically modified for those members of large hierarchical organizations who are seen as the future management. Private industry is replete with development programs for management trainees, and these efforts find their counterparts in government and in the military. Development efforts include rotation between assignments, coaching, and formal courses both inside and outside the organization. The effects of these efforts are still debatable. A recent comprehensive evaluation of research on the results of management development programs (Campbell, Dunnette, Lawler, and Weick, 1970) has concluded that their value is still very much in doubt. It is possible to assert without fear of scientific contradiction that managers merely find their proper level, given the opportunity, and that there are no significant changes in basic management ability after graduation from college.

This lack of knowledge has implications not only for the efficacy of development programs but also for the design of the programs themselves. How is it possible to seek to affect development without knowing the laws of that development and how it proceeds, if it does, in the absence of intervention? Should there be, for example, a program for making young men more ambitious, or do most of them naturally become so as they acquire the obligations of a home and family? Do dependent young men become more independent when given a challenging job? Should they be gradually coached into independence? Is it hopeless no matter what is done? These and a myriad of other questions cannot be answered and, in fact, are never even asked by most management developers. As White points out, "The scientist has almost never studied ordinary people as they increase their mastery over the ordinary problems of daily life."

The Management Progress Study, which provides the data for this book, is a study of growth and development during the adult years. Its subjects are men who early in their work lives became part of the management of a large private enterprise. Due to the time in history when these recruits were hired as potential middle managers, the sample contains no women or blacks. Because of the particular organization into which recruits were hired—the Bell System—one might suggest that the recruits would be different in a small business, in an educational institution, a profession, or some other occupational setting. The subjects and the setting, nevertheless, are fairly typical of millions of managers in large enterprises; thus our participants represent a segment of the population crucial to the well-being of our society.

ORIGINS OF THE STUDY

The Study grew out of practical concerns. The Bell System recruits as many as 2000 college graduates a year. Some of these individuals pursue careers as scientists and technicians, but most are expected to enter the stream of general management and rise to the middle and upper levels. In addition, the telephone companies in the System promote about 10,000 men and women from the ranks each year. Although the majority remain in the lower levels of management, many eventually compete with the college recruits for higher positions.

The Bell System has had a long history of concern with management development. After World War II, and particularly during the 1950s, this concern blossomed into an imposing array of programs. Promising middle managers attended the University of Pennsylvania for an entire academic year, shorter programs were worked out with such leading colleges as Dartmouth and Williams, and an ambitious in-house program of several weeks' duration was devised for department heads. In addition, many training packages of two to five days were attended by thousands of foremen, chief operators, and district and division managers.

Robert K. Greenleaf, who in the middle 1950s was Director of both Management Development and Management Research, was aware of the lack of basic knowledge of growth and development in adult life. With the Bell System making such heavy investments in its management, he became convinced that a significant commitment should be made to basic research. He persuaded higher management to institute a study of young managers in the business as their careers unfolded, and he employed Douglas W. Bray to design and carry out the research.

The Management Progress Study was started with several general questions in mind:

- What significant changes take place in men as their lives develop in a business context?
- Conversely, are there changes we might expect or desire that do not occur?

- What are the causes of these changes or stabilities? More particularly, what are the effects of company climate, policies, and practices?

These general questions subsume a large number of more specific inquiries. The following will suggest the wealth of possibilities:

- Does learning ability decline as people grow older?
- Do interests widen or narrow with age?
- Are young men more materialistic than older men?
- Is face-to-face leadership an enduring trait?
- At what point does drive for advancement slack off?
- Do less successful men devote more time to their families and outside activities?
- Are health problems more frequent among the upwardly mobile or among those at a dead end?
- Should a new management recruit be brought along gradually or thrust into an early challenge?
- Why do some men leave a company even when they are doing well?
- How realistic are managers in evaluating their own potential?
- Do people become more concerned with others as they grow older?
- Does personality adjustment have anything to do with success?

Although the Management Progress Study was conceptualized as a study of development, it was inevitable that the Study would have implications for selection of managers. Therefore, an additional general question was:

- How accurately can progress in management be predicted? What are the important indicators and how are they best measured?

THE DESIGN OF THE STUDY

The design of the Study was guided by several considerations. First, it was necessary to ensure that the subjects' abilities, motivation, and other characteristics when first measured would be those brought with them to management, uninfluenced by experience in management. This meant that college recruits should be evaluated for the Study as soon as possible after employment, when they were just starting their careers in management.

As a second guideline, it was decided that the subjects should represent the two broad sources of telephone company middle and upper management—college graduates recruited with middle management as the goal and noncollege lower level managers who had emerged from the vocational ranks and might compete for higher level management positions. Approximately two-thirds of the subjects, therefore, were college recruits, the remainder being young noncollege managers. Only the first of these groups, the college recruits, is covered in this volume. A later companion report will present the findings for those who rose from the ranks.

It was further decided that to specify the nature and degree of changes in the subjects over the years, it would be necessary to examine them thoroughly from time to time. Interviews and questionnaires would not be adequate; a full battery of tests and interviews, supplemented by other methods of evaluation would be required. A three-and-one-half day "assessment center" was devised, and it was planned to put the subjects through this extensive appraisal at the start of the Study, again eight years later, once again twenty years from the start, and probably one or more additional times after that.

In addition to this assessment at various points of life, it was felt necessary to keep in touch with the subject and his career on an annual basis. The plan, therefore, was to interview the subject annually and to interview those in his telephone company who were in a position to comment on him and his career at about the same time. Table 1 outlines the design of the Study for its first eight years, the years covered by this book.

Because the assessment center (described in detail in Chapter 3) could handle only twelve subjects a week, and since assessment

Table I   Design of the Management Progress Study

Time Period	Data from Subjects	Data from Subjects' Companies
Start	Assessment	—
Elapsed years		
1–4	Intensive interview Questionnaires of attitudes and expectations	Intensive interview with departmental personnel supervisor
5	Intensive interview Questionnaires of attitudes and expectations	Intensive interview with departmental personnel supervisor Interviews with two former bosses
6	Intensive interview Questionnaires of attitudes and expectations	Intensive interview with present boss
7	Intensive interview Questionnaires of attitudes and expectations	—
8	Reassessment	Collection of present appraisal, level, and salary information

staffs were available only in the summer months, initial inclusion of subjects in the Study spread over five calendar years. For the college recruits, the subjects of this book, these were the summers of 1956, 1957, 1959, and 1960. In the first three years the subjects were the college recruits of the Michigan Bell, Chesapeake and Potomac, and Bell of Pennsylvania Telephone Companies, respectively. In the last year the college recruits of the Northwestern and Mountain Bell Companies were covered. In each company all the college recruits of that recruiting year who had reported for work

Table 2   College Recruit Subjects of Management
Progress Study

Year	Telephone Company	Number of Recruits
1956	Michigan	67
1957	Chesapeake and Potomac	79
1959	Pennsylvania	56
1960	Northwestern	36
	Mountain	36
	Total	274

by the time assessment was under way were included; there was no sampling. Table 2 presents this information and gives the number of recruits from each company. There were 274 recruits in all.

A final consideration—confidentiality—was important not only with respect to possible ethical implications, but also from the research point of view. Frank cooperation could hardly be expected from the subjects if they feared that information about them would be given to others in the company. Other respondents, such as personnel men and supervisors, would also be reluctant to make negative statements about the subjects and would be very unlikely to be outspoken in evaluating the subjects' bosses. Most serious, no unbiased study of careers in progress would be achieved if the study information itself influenced those careers.

Although the Study is now in its eighteenth year, confidentiality has been perfectly preserved. All Study data on individuals are identified only by code numbers, which were assigned at the start of the Study. No identifiable information on individuals has ever been revealed to anyone except the researchers. Even the subjects have received no feedback on Study findings pertaining to themselves as individuals. Finally, the Fels Research Institute on the campus of Antioch College has made a major contribution by serving since the start of the Study in 1956 as the repository of the complete file of Study data.

Thus the Study set out to fill in some of the gaps in our knowledge of adult development and to deal with many unanswered questions about causes and effects of success and lack of success in a management career. This book is a comprehensive presentation of the results of that Study for the first eight years in the business life of the college recruits. More than 40 percent failed to last out this period; of those who remained, some have already come to a dead end, while others are clearly on their way to the top.

2

RECRUITMENT AND ACCEPTANCE

Tens of thousands of young men graduate every year from America's colleges and universities, and a substantial fraction of these individuals wind up several months later as management trainees in medium and large business corporations. Some are hired in the belief that the courses they have pursued in college, such as engineering, accounting, or business administration, will be directly relevant to the aims of the company that employs them. In other cases, courses taken may be seen as having little direct significance, but graduation from college is considered to indicate the presence of intelligence and motivation that can be directed to the hiring company's purposes. In any case, the "better" college graduates are eagerly sought by business and, in turn, many college graduates look forward to employment with a firm that will offer an attractive mixture of challenge, opportunity, and security.

The process by which the many graduates are assorted among the many companies that eventually employ them takes different forms. Some graduates, attracted by advertising, the general reputation of a firm, or suggestions of friends or relatives, may take the initiative and apply directly for employment. Others may reach the employment office through an employment agency. Those entering the business through these routes are called "over-the-counter" hires in Bell System parlance, to distinguish them from the "campus recruits." The latter are those with whom the first contact is made by a company representative who visits the college campus.

Campus recruiting is, of course, a competitive activity in which each participating business attempts to secure the best possible group of graduates. In years when the demand is high, some firms may experience difficulty in merely getting on the placement officer's schedule to set up shop on a particular campus, and even the most prestigious company is limited to a twenty-minute initial interview with the candidate. In good times, some seniors may interview with fifteen to twenty companies and receive offers from ten or twelve.

BELL SYSTEM COLLEGE RECRUITING

Organized interviewing on college campuses was begun by some Bell System companies as early as the beginning of World War I, and a coordinated plan was established in 1922. The plan has undergone development and improvement ever since. In brief, the campus visit is made by a Bell System team consisting of representatives from one or more telephone companies, the Western Electric Company, and Bell Telephone Laboratories. The telephone company in whose territory a particular college or university is located serves as the host and coordinator of the team.

The amount of information on which the recruiter bases his judgment of the candidate varies, depending on the energy and resources of the recruiter. At the least it includes information from the application form and from a brief interview. This material is often supplemented by data from the registrar's office, and facts and opinions from faculty members and placement officers. (Nowadays a mental ability test is standard practice, but this was not true when the Management Progress Study was started.)

The candidate who appears promising on the basis of the initial interview and other available information is given another more intensive interview, often the next day. Although this interview is also the basis for some further judgments by the interviewer, much of it is devoted to answering the candidate's inquiries and persuading him of the desirability of Bell System employment. In some of the Bell telephone companies, the second campus interview may result in a final decision to make the employment offer. In most cases, however, a visit to the company and further interviewing are required.

The recruiter's judgment is exercised against the background of considerable Bell System research conducted over the years on the relationships between college achievement and later success in the company. This research was initiated in the 1920s by Donald S. Bridgman, who had much to do with the development of the entire Bell System recruiting program. The results were first publicized in 1928 in an article by the then president of AT&T, Walter S. Gifford, in an article in *Harper's Magazine* entitled "Does Business Want Scholars?" and a little later by Bridgman in a more detailed treatment: "Success in College and Business " (Gifford, 1928; Bridgman, 1930).

These early studies demonstrated that rank in college graduating class was a valid predictor of success in the company. Almost twice as many of those in the top third of their graduating classes as those in the lowest third were found to be clearly successful. Success was defined as being in the top third of salary, compared with those having equal years of service with the company. The exact figures were as follows: 45 percent of the academic top third was in the top salary third, versus 22 percent of those in the lowest academic third.

The other clear predictor appearing in the early studies was achievement in such campus activities as college publications, class or club leadership, and team management. Those with substantial campus achievement were later found in the top salary third 43 percent of the time, as compared with 28 percent of those having no campus achievement.

This predictive research was repeated on a much larger scale in the 1950s with remarkably similar results, and once again the findings were brought to public attention by an AT&T president. Frederick R. Kappel made the study the basis of a Greene Foundation lecture entitled "From the World of College to the World of Work" (Kappel, 1962). The second study came too late, however, to have any influence on the hiring of the college graduates in the Management Progress Study.

It might be deduced from the foregoing that the 274 college graduates who made up the college recruit sample of the Management Progress Study had been hired on the basis of almost identical standards, even though they had been hired by five different telephone companies in four different years. This was really not the case. AT&T college employment recommendations were not binding on the individual telephone companies, and they were not equally accepted by all companies. Moreover, the recommendations that were accepted were not always well implemented.

Recruiting teams varied greatly among the five telephone companies in the Management Progress Study, both in their numbers and in their training. In one company two full-time, experienced men from the central personnel department were supplemented by others from the operating departments. In another the recruiters were assigned only to schools of which they were alumni. Another company used men only from the operating departments. Recruiters varied from second to fifth level managers (in a seven-level organization). Selection of recruiters was informal, and training varied from minimal to quite intensive.

The scope of Bell System college recruiting is suggested by some data from the recruiting year of 1956, the year in which the Management Progress Study was started. In that year approximately 2300 college graduates were hired by the System as a whole; of these, 1500 were hired by the telephone companies (as distinct from Western Electric and Bell Telephone Laboratories). Michigan Bell, the first participant in the Study, employed 75; only 37 were recruited on campus, however, and the remainder either applied directly or were returnees from military service.

During the recruiting year Michigan Bell recruiters visited 20 campuses and interviewed 608 applicants; about one-third of these (209) were invited to visit the company. The company finally made offers to 79, and 33 accepted. The remaining four men of the 37 campus recruits were referred by recruiters in other telephone companies.

The Bell System recruiting apparatus thus operates to offer jobs to hundreds of young men out of the thousands it sees at least initially on college campuses. Of those who do receive an offer, approximately one-half accept. The recruits in the Management Progress Study were, of course, among those who had decided to accept.

REASONS FOR ACCEPTING EMPLOYMENT

Why did they accept? The subjects were asked this question at the assessment center, both in interviews and in written form. From answers, categorized into five groupings in Table 3, it can be seen that the most frequent reason given has to do with opportunities for challenge and development. There was a widespread belief that the Bell System would help one develop into an effective manager and would move one along rapidly as this development occurred. More than half also mentioned other characteristics of the company, such as its size, employee benefit plans, and location. These and other reasons are illustrated in the following quotes from assessment center materials:

> I was interviewed by nine companies. I chose Bell because it is a large company. It is big business at its best. I was impressed with the calibre of the Bell System men I met. They have great ability and seem to be very honest and sincere. I was also attracted to the training program. My advisors in college told me that even if I didn't make it with the System, I wouldn't have lost anthing because the training would be worth it in itself.

> The Bell System is large. It hires hundreds of college men each year to replace the men who retire. Bell offers a fine training program and has future rewards worth striving for. Money, promotion, interesting work, good fellow workers, and prestige; all these I can get if I try.

> I decided that the Bell System provided more than any other firm, including: better overall benefits; security, good

Table 3   Reasons Given for Accepting Bell System Employment

Reason	Recruits Mentioning (%)
Extrinsic Characteristics of the Firm vis à vis the Employee (e.g., geographic location, income, benefits, limited geographic mobility required, security, size of firm, recruiting policies . . .)	55
Characteristics of the Firm vis à vis the Larger Community (e.g., prestigious company, serves the community and the nation, high ethical standards . . .)	17
Intrinsic Characteristics—Work Related (e.g., training program, employee–management development policy, work offers challenge, personal development, opportunity for advancement, opportunity for self-expression . . .)	80
Intrinsic Characteristics—People Related (e.g., supervisor–employee relations, interesting people, morale . . .)	32
Influence from Relevant Others or Direct Experience with Company (e.g., mother or father worked with company, summer job with company . . .)	24

working conditions, friendly associates, better opportunity for advancement, encouragement of advanced study, excellent training program.

Although there were many lengthy answers and all the recruits furnished a plausible reason for joining the company, many gave the impression that they were merely producing socially acceptable words without much substance behind them. After all, a person *should* be able to say why he has made an important decision! But when one has just come out of college and has never been inside most of the companies that interview him, how can one be sure? All recruiters are likely to present their firms as full of opportunities and rewards. Behind all the wordy reasons given for choosing Bell, it may be that there lurked much doubt and hope. Perhaps the following comment expressed the feelings of many besides the young man who actually said it:

> What I want in a career I really don't know. I don't know what I'm suited for. I like people. The Bell System takes a boy and gives him a varied program. Your qualities will come out and eventually you'll be placed where you fit.

3

THE ASSESSMENT CENTER

During World War II many military and civilian candidates for assignments in America's intelligence organization, the Office of Strategic Services (OSS), were held incommunicado for a week on a farm near Washington, D.C. There they underwent an imaginative and taxing series of interviews, tests, and performance simulations designed to reveal whether they had the qualities needed for intelligence work. The candidates were examined not only for mental ability and motivation to serve but for physical stamina, emotional stability, resistance to stress, and many other characteristics. To this end they were sent over obstacle courses, attacked in stress interviews, and observed when they were falsely told they had flunked out—the week was calculated to reveal every asset and weakness they might have (OSS Staff, 1948).

This assessment center, as it was called, was staffed by a group of well-trained psychologists and psychiatrists under the direction of Dr. Henry A. Murray of Harvard University. Murray's pioneering work in the 1930s, published under the title *Explorations in Personality* (Murray, 1938), had paved the way for such global evaluations of human characteristics and potential. That Murray and his associates felt it necessary to observe candidates for several days and to put them through elaborate individual and group performance situations implied the conviction that ordinary interviews and standard paper-and-pencil psychological tests were insufficient to fully assess an individual.

To carry out the plan of the Management Progress Study, it was necessary to determine as completely as possible the abilities, potential, motivation, attitudes, and personality characteristics of each subject at the time he started in the Study. As the various qualities that would have to be evaluated were decided on and techniques for measuring them were selected or devised, it became clear that only a small number of subjects could be appraised at a time and that they would have to be examined for several days. The planners realized that an assessment center would have to be devised and implemented.

THE MANAGEMENT PROGRESS VARIABLES

Three sources were used in developing the list of personal attributes, called the Management Progress Variables, which the assessment center would seek to measure. One was the management and psychological literature, which suggested many qualities that had been shown (or more often merely hypothesized) to be important in managerial success. Other variables were proposed by several behavioral scientists outside the Bell System. The third source—senior personnel executives inside the System—were asked to think not only of qualities important to success but also of qualities that might be changed by experience in the telephone company. A long list of qualities couched in several different vocabularies was amassed. The senior author of this book reconciled the many differences and settled on the 25 attributes listed below.

1. *Scholastic Aptitude* (general mental ability)
2. *Oral Communication Skill*
   How good would this man be in presenting an oral report to a small conference group on a subject he knew well?
   Written Communication Skill
   How good would this man be in composing a communicative and formally correct memorandum on a subject he knew well?

3. *Human Relations Skills*

How effectively can this man lead a group to accomplish a task without arousing hostility?

4. *Personal Impact*

How forceful and likable an early impression does this man make?

5. *Perception of Threshold Social Cues*

How readily does this man perceive minimal cues in the behavior of others toward him?

6. *Creativity*

How likely is this man to solve a management problem in a novel way?

7. *Self-Objectivity*

How realistic a view does this man have of his own assets and liabilities, and how much insight does he have into his own motives?

8. *Social Objectivity*

How free is this man from prejudices against racial, ethnic, socio-economic, educational, and other kinds of groups?

9. *Behavior Flexibility*

How readily can this man, when motivated, modify his behavior to reach a goal?

10. *Need Approval of Superiors*

To what extent is this man emotionally dependent on authority figures?

11. *Need Approval of Peers*

To what extent is this man emotionally dependent on like and lower status associates?

12. *Inner Work Standards*

To what extent will this man want to do a good job even if a less good one is acceptable to his boss and others?

13. *Need Advancement*

To what extent does this man need to be promoted significantly earlier than his peers?

14. *Need Security*

To what extent does this man need a secure job?

15. *Goal Flexibility*

To what extent will this man be able to change his life goals in accordance with reality opportunities?

16. *Primacy of Work*

To what extent will this man find satisfactions from work more important than satisfactions from other areas of life?

17. *Bell System Value Orientation*

To what extent is this man likely to incorporate Bell System values, such as service, friendliness, and justice of company position on earnings, rates, and wages?

18. *Realism of Expectations*

To what extent do this man's expectations about his work life with the company conform to what is likely to be true?

19. *Tolerance of Uncertainty*

To what extent will this man's work performance stand up under uncertain or unstructured conditions?

20. *Ability to Delay Gratification*

To what extent will this man be able to work over long periods without great rewards in order to reach later rewards?

21. *Resistance to Stress*

To what extent will this man's work performance stand up in the face of personal stress?

22. *Range of Interests*

To what extent is this man interested in a variety of fields of activity, such as science, politics, sports, music, and art?

23. *Energy*

How continuously can this man sustain a high level of work activity?

24. *Organization and Planning*

How effectively can this man organize his work, and how well does he plan ahead?

25. *Decision Making*

How ready is this man to make decisions, and how good are the decisions he makes?

THE BUSINESS GAME

"You are about to go into business together. That is, in working on this problem you are to pretend that you are partners in a small manufacturing enterprise. As partners you operate a small shop that makes toys for Christmas sale." These words, read to a group of six young men who had donned colored vests for purposes of identification, started one of the several assessment exercises that, together, would give the assessment staff the observations on which to base their judgments.*

The assessment exercises were of several types. Some of the more usual, which are not described in detail, were tests of general mental ability, personality and attitude questionnaires, and the interview. Others were group problems, an individual administrative exercise, and projective tests of personality. All told, the assessment occupied three-and-one-half days for each group of subjects.

In the toy manufacturing problem, the assessees had to buy the parts for simple toys, assemble them, and sell them back, with the goal of making as much money as possible. Group action was necessary; no one could buy or sell as an individual. The problem was divided into six periods for a total of approximately two hours. Prices of parts and amounts for which assembled toys would be purchased changed sharply from period to period, and good organization was necessary to show a profit. The group was given three dollars to start with and was allowed to keep anything they were able to make. This occasionally went as high as seven or eight dollars.

The Manufacturing Problem was intended to elicit behavior that would be helpful primarily in judging the following items from the list of 25 variables just defined: Human Relations Skills, Self-Objectivity (from comparison of the subject's view of his own performance, gained from a questionnaire administered at the end of the problem, with the view of his peers and the staff observers), Behavior Flexibility, Need Approval of Peers, Tolerance of Uncertainty, Resistance to Stress, Energy, Organization and Planning, and Decision Making.

Participation in the problem was observed by two staff members who took many notes and later prepared a comprehensive analytical report of each man's performance. Here is a condensation of one such report:

This young man's forcefulness and persistence paid off in the Manufacturing Problem, where he emerged as the un-

* This business game was contributed to the Study by John K. Hemphill.

named but clear leader by the time the Problem was over. He was verbally active and kept up a steady flow of rather directive suggestions and orders which his peers came to follow. He was challenged for group leadership only once and succeeded in outtalking his opponent. Athough he made most of the production decisions himself, he delegated most of the other jobs. His ideas on how to increase group efficiency, although not highly original, proved correct and resulted in a profit for the group. He seemed capable of organizing his peers well and kept their output level high without loss of morale. The candidate tended to underestimate his contributions; his self-description questionnaire suggests that he did not grasp the extent to which his actions influenced the group.

THE GROUP DISCUSSION PROBLEM

The other group problem at the assessment center was quite different. "For this session," the candidates (again a group of six) were told, "you are to consider yourself a middle management person in the Bell System. Each of you has a number of first level foremen in his organization. A foreman is to be promoted to fill a vacancy at second level. Each of you has looked over your own foremen and has selected a man you consider to be the most qualified to get this promotion. In a moment I will give you a description of the man you have selected."

Each of the six assessees was given a 300-word summary of the background and strengths and weaknesses of the foreman he was to champion in the session to follow. The assessee was told to study this summary for ten minutes without taking notes, then he was given five more minutes to prepare a presentation on behalf of his candidate. In the oral presentation period that followed, each assessee was called on to speak for no more than five minutes on his candidate; questions were not allowed at that point.

When the presentations were concluded, the group was told that they now had one hour for free discussion to select one of the six foremen to receive the promotion. They were also instructed to rank all six foremen in case other vacancies arose. The assessees were told: "Because you will be judged on your skill in arguing for your man, you should try to convince your peers that your candidate is well qualified for promotion. As a group, however, you will want to select the candidate who will make the greatest contribution to your company."

The Group Discussion Problem was intended to reveal qualities such as Oral Communication Skill, Human Relations Skills, Perception of Social Cues, Self-Objectivity (through a self-rating questionnaire), Behavior Flexibility, Need Approval of Peers, Resistance to Stress, Energy, and Organizing and Planning.

The staff reports of performance in the Group Discussion covered, of course, both the Oral Presentation and the Discussion stages. Here is a summary of one man's presentation:

> This man's oral presentation was below average. He made clucking sounds with his tongue throughout, used "uhs" frequently, and did a good deal of throat clearing. He looked around at the group, but his eye contact was only sporadic. He seemed quite ill-at-ease. He was the first to make a clear mention that his candidate did have a fault. He did this rather ineptly. In discussing one of his candidate's "qualifications" he made a lengthy point about machines and tools; the point was more confusing than effective. His speech closed apologetically with "So I hope you'll consider John for the job."

A different candidate performed somewhat more effectively in the discussion stage:

> He was the first to speak and seemed intent on drawing positive attention to his candidate. His efforts to do so, however, were rebuffed several times by one of the more aggressive group members and the trainee seemed somewhat stressed by these attacks. He sometimes withdrew when confronted with criticism of his candidate, but at other times defended his man effectively. On one occasion he challenged his attacker and aggressively questioned him concerning the foreman he represented. During all the discussion, the trainee indicated greater concern with trying

to sell his man than with the organization and progress of the group.

THE IN-BASKET

The group exercises just described tested the assessee in face-to-face interactions with his peers. The In-Basket* was designed to reveal how he would handle real management problems entirely on his own.

You are now Mr. C. D. Evans, Plant Superintendent of the East District in Division A of the Green Area of the Eastern Telephone Company. You have just arrived in your new job. Mr. I. W. Prior, your predecessor, died suddenly of a heart attack last Wednesday, March 28. You were notified Friday at 4 P.M. of your new appointment but you could not get here until today, Sunday, April 1.

Today is your first day on your new job and here is what your secretary has left for you. Since it is Sunday no one else is around and you cannot reach anyone on the telephone. You must leave in exactly three hours to catch a plane for an important meeting connected with your previous assignment. You will not be able to take along anything to work on. The meeting will keep you away both Monday and Tuesday. You are working Sunday afternoon because you want to take care of anything that might need your attention before Wednesday. In the large envelope in front of you you will find three packets. One contains an organization chart, a map of the district and of the division, a copy of the management guide, and a copy of the union contract. The second packet contains the materials your secretary has left on your desk for your attention. These materials include letters, reports, memoranda, etc. Your secretary has attached materials from the files to some of the documents. The third packet contains a copy of the instructions I am

---

* The In-Basket was constructed by Educational Testing Service working with AT&T's Management Training Section.

now reading, office forms, memo pads, pencils, and paper.
You can use these materials to write letters, memos, notes
to yourself, etc.

The paragraphs just quoted are the significant parts of the instructions read to the assessees as they started the challenging "In-
Basket." When they inspected the materials their new secretary,
Rose Right, had accumulated for them, they found 25 distinct but
interrelated items. These ranged from minor but thorny problems,
such as a note from Rose Right herself that she had made all
arrangements for a vacation starting in one week, to a rather complicated engineering report on which the assessee's new boss wanted
a response on Wednesday morning. The assessee was instructed to
take any actions he thought he should take, schedule and outline
any meetings he might want to have, write notes requesting information, delegate action, and so on.

Shortly after completing his three-hour work period, the assessee
was interviewed intensively by a member of the assessment staff.
The interviewer sought to learn exactly how the assessee had
tackled his work in terms of such areas as overall organization,
priorities, and handling interrelationships among the items. In
addition, he wanted to find out what perception the assessee had of
the general situation in the district in terms of what he was able to
learn from the materials presented. Finally, and most important, he
tried to dig into the reasoning the assessee had followed in the
action, or lack of action, with which he had responded to each
item. More specific variables that the interviewer had in mind
were Written Communication Skill, Human Relations Skills, Creativity, Need Approval of Superiors, Inner Work Standards, Tolerance of Uncertainty, Resistance to Stress, Energy, Organizing and
Planning, and Decision Making.

In-Basket reports prepared by the assessment staff were often
quite lengthy, going into considerable detail about the more important variables. The following excerpt is a view of one assessee's
decision making:

This man is low in decision making. Practically all his
'decisions' were to get more information, file the item, or

to take the item up in the future with the people involved. He wanted to interview several people. He asked Rose Right to file an important letter, the absence report, the productive hours report, training and overtime reports, etc., even though some of these clearly suggest remedial action. He held three other items for more information, which left very few items on which he took any direct action at all.

THE PROJECTIVE TESTS

The three assessment exercises discussed so far—the Manufacturing Problem, the Group Discussion, and the In-Basket—were designed to assist in evaluating a recruit's management ability and potential by direct observation of his performance when confronted by managerial situations. The projective tests were quite different. They were intended to discover important aspects of a man's motivational and personality characteristics by an analysis of his free responses to pictures and words. (Projective tests are so named because the stimuli they put before the subject can call forth any of a large number of possible responses. The subject can therefore "project" his own meaning into them, revealing something about himself by what he projects.)

One of the projective tests used at the assessment center was the well-known Thematic Apperception Test, developed many years ago by the same Henry Murray who later directed the OSS assessment centers. In this test, the subject is shown a series of pictures and is asked to tell (or in the present case, write) a story about what is happening in the picture, what led up to the events described, and what the outcome will be. Because of time limitations, only six of the pictures were used.

The other projective tests were two incomplete sentences tests. In these the subject is given the start of a sentence and asked to finish it. One of the tests used was the commercially available Rotter Incomplete Sentences Blank;* the other was a Management Incomplete Sentences Test developed especially for the Manage-

* Published by The Psychological Corporation, New York, N.Y.

ment Progress Study by Walter Katkovsky. Here are some of the sentence stems with which the recruits were confronted:

To me, failure is_____

A large company_____

When I compare myself with others_____

A clinical psychologist reviewed all the responses produced by each recruit to the two sets of incomplete sentences and to the six pictures. He then wrote an analytical report focusing on insights of importance relative to a management career. The following are excerpts from several of these reports:

> This young man appears to be a mild, easygoing person who does little thinking and planning concerning his life and generally tries to adjust to circumstances as they occur to the best of his ability.
>
> While he states that a secure job is not what he is looking for, two of his responses suggest that he fears the risk and instability of being on the open market. Thus, he states, " THE WORST THAT COULD HAPPEN is that I lose my job."
>
> As a supervisor of others, the trainee probably feels uneasy and awkward. In a sense he lacks the maturity and stability to be a successful or competent leader. He has to fight a tendency to be dominated by other people, and he counters this by seeing things through which would better be delegated to a subordinate. So, when things go wrong, he feels directly responsible and blames himself. His major supervisory tactic seems to be to get his subordinates to like him and thereby give him their faithful support and best efforts.
>
> Competitive situations promote his desire for self-improvement, and it seems likely that he participates in activities designed to advance his abilities and confidence to a moderate extent. He expresses interest in reading, politics and world events and probably is a moderately thoughtful

person. His opinions seem conforming but tolerant and flexible.

THE INTERVIEW

During his time at the assessment center, each recruit underwent an interview lasting from one and one-half to two hours. The session was loosely structured, with each interviewer free to vary the approach according to his own style and his perceptions of what would work best with a specific recruit. Subjects usually discussed included educational background, extracurricular activities, reasons for joining the Bell System, expectations for the future, religious and political interests, and hobbies.

The interviewer's task was not to elicit any particular set of facts but to secure material of probable help in judging characteristics such as self-objectivity, realism of expectations, need advancement, and range of interests. The interview was not recorded; the interviewer took notes as he went along. Immediately following the session, the schedule allowed the interviewer free time to organize his notes and to write or dictate his report.

THE CONTEMPORARY AFFAIRS TEST

In addition to the three major simulations, the projective tests, and an interview, the recruits took mental ability tests and filled out several questionnaires that measured certain aspects of personality and attitude. Although the rest of these instruments are not described at this point, the Contemporary Affairs Test deserves special mention. This 120-item test, which was revised and standardized yearly, measured the recruit's knowledge of what had happened recently in national and international affairs, science and medicine, the arts, and sports. Here are some sample items from the tests developed in the late 1950s:

What was the accusation made concerning the National Guard by Secretary of Defense Wilson during 1957?
A. The National Guard is totally unprepared.

B. That National Guardsmen were like "kennel-fed dogs."
C. Draft dodging by means of the National Guard was a scandal.
D. That members of the National Guard had not been good soldiers in Korea.

Explorer VI was successfully orbited from its launching site at Cape Canaveral. The "paddlewheel" design of this satellite allows it to:

A. Take advantage of the prevailing jet stream of its orbital plane.
B. Make use of solar energy to charge its transmitter.
C. Achieve greater speed in its orbital plane.
D. Overcome the danger of gradual rusting.

The composer of the sound track for the moving picture **Anatomy of a Murder** was:

A. Duke Ellington
B. Henry Mancini
C. Dimitri Tiomkin
D. Leonard Bernstein

THE ASSESSMENT STAFF CONFERENCE

By the time three and one-half days had passed, most of the assessees felt that they had been very thoroughly examined indeed. Some— surprisingly enough, since they were given no information about how they had done—said they had learned a lot about themselves during the long series of tests and exercises. At the dinner that topped off the assessment process for each group of recruits, the great majority were in good spirits and clearly willing to continue in the Study. They departed with much handshaking and many "Thank you's" on both sides.

The assessment staff spent the rest of the work week in the analysis of the performance of each recruit. The first order of business was to score the tests and to complete detailed written reports of the performance of each assessee in the interview, the Manufacturing Problem, the Group Discussion, the In-Basket, and the projective tests. The final day and a half of the week was devoted to a meeting of the assessment staff during which each recruit was reviewed and rated. The discussion of each man took from 60 to 90 minutes, depending on the complexity of the case. All reports and test scores were read aloud by the staff member responsible, with the others taking such notes as they felt they would require for rating purposes. This done, each of the staff rated the recruit on the 25 Management Progress Variables listed earlier in this chapter. Rating was on a five-point scale—a rating of 5 meaning that the assessee had a great deal of the quality; 1, that he had very little of it. In case of serious disagreement among the raters, a more detailed discussion of the variable on which they differed took place, more evidence was examined, and consensus usually emerged.

THE ASSESSMENT SUMMARY

Although the discussion session just described completed the work of the staff at the time of assessment, one more step had to be taken before the assessment file was deemed to be complete. During the months that followed, all the materials on each assessee were carefully reviewed and a lengthy summary was written by a clinical psychologist. These reports usually ran about five single-spaced pages; they served to encapsulate the recruit at the time he started in the Study. The following excerpts from the summary of the performance of a promising young man will suggest the scope of these reports:

> This trainee was 24 years of age at the time of his attendance at the assessment center. He had just joined the Telephone Company immediately following his graduation from the University. Both his appearance and behavior left the impression that he is a mild individual lacking in forcefulness. At the same time, his manner was always serious, matter-of-fact and diligently oriented to the problem at hand. He cooperated fully on all the assessment techniques and appeared highly motivated to do as good a job as

possible. In fact, there were several indications from his behavior that his strong desire to make a favorable impression promoted above average tenseness in the assessment situation. On several occasions his behavior was characterized by nervousness and controlled quietness, as though he were reluctant to enter into a situation until he felt absolutely sure of himself. Although he was not very outgoing, his approach to others was aways friendly and accepting. While he was evaluated favorably on several of the assessment techniques, most members of the staff felt that his overall impact was no more than average because of his tense, restrained and rather reticent manner.

This young man's view of the Bell System was a highly favorable one at the time of the assessment and it seemed quite probable that he would identify with the values of the company rather quickly. He expressed considerable enthusiasm and motivation for assuming management responsibilities and indicated a confident attitude concerning the future. He stated that he was interested in working closely with others and that he was willing to compete and apply himself fully in order to succeed in his work. In actuality, however, the trainee left the impression that he had little knowledge of the specific activities associated with a management role and of his exact qualifications for such a position. Rather, the picture he created was that of a young man who was eager to cooperate, comply and do his best in order to fulfill the expectations others had for him. His concern with advancement and general need achievement appeared average for the group. He stated that he would like to reach the third level of management in five or six years, but he was uncertain about his desire for advancement beyond this level. While the general rewards of higher level management positions were attractive to him, he thought that the demands of such positions may be more extensive than he would like.

In most respects, the trainee's general abilities compare favorably with the total sample of men in the Management

Progress Study. His use of language is very good, both in written and oral work, and he expresses his ideas in a clear, succinct fashion. His ability to deal with quantitative materials also is above average. The only weak aspect of his performance on the achievement tests administered at the center was in contemporary affairs, where he fell below average for the group. His performance on the In-Basket was characterized by a high degree of motivation, seriousness and ability to tackle the items with thought and organization. While the report on his work on the test makes no specific evaluations of his decision-making skills, it is noted that he verbalized the importance of maintaining a philosophy of management which stresses the training and development of subordinates, delegating responsibilities and working through lines of organization. Both his human relations skills and his perception of social cues were rated above average.

Although the trainee was one of the more quiet members in the group projects, he succeeded in making a very favorable impression. This was particularly true in the Manufacturing Problem where he emerged as the leader in the middle part of the problem. Initially, he was quiet, but very attentive while another group member assumed the leadership role in an authoritarian manner. Later, when this group member lost his influence and abdicated the leadership position, the trainee quickly became the person to whom others looked for direction. As his leadership was acknowledged, he became increasingly active both verbally and physically. He conferred with the other group members on their activities and clarified the assignments and roles each member was to fulfill. While the calibre of his ideas seemed no more than average, his ability to handle the problems which arose was quite satisfactory. His success in the group seemed to be a function of his willingness to work hard, his adaptable nature and the fact that he always expressed himself clearly. He also demonstrated excellent ability to work with others. His democratic style of leading served to increase his influence in the group.

The trainee was less active in the Group Discussion, but again demonstrated a high degree of perceptiveness, good oral communications skills and effective planning ability. He spoke only twice during the first 25 minutes of the Group Discussion, both times to ask other members questions about their candidates. He did this in an astute and tactful way. Later, he answered the questions of others about the man he represented with conviction and good knowledge of his candidate. His major contribution came during the voting, when the trainee suggested that they use a secret ballot and rank the candidates in order of preference. In evaluating the trainee's performance in this situation, the two observers differed a great deal. One observer saw him as only an average group member because of the relatively few comments he made during the discussion. The other observer, however, gave the trainee the top ranking in spite of his relatively quiet and unaggressive behavior. He was favorably impressed with the trainee's ability to defend his candidate and with the two key procedural suggestions he made concerning the voting. There was also some difference of opinion by the observers in the evaluation of the trainee's formal oral presentation. One observer rated him only average because of his apparent nervousness, whereas the other observer gave him the highest possible rating, arguing that his nervousness didn't detract from the effectiveness of his talk. The trainee was described as having spoken slowly and emphatically, maintaining good eye contact with the audience and handling his materials in an organized and knowledgable way.

Most members of the staff anticipated a very successful career in the Bell System for the trainee. The general feeling was that he will remain with the System, will develop a strong sense of affiliation with the values and purposes of the telephone company and will derive considerable personal satisfaction from his work. There was a mild amount of disagreement concerning the speed with which he is likely to reach the district level of management. Only one member of the staff thought that his advancement to the third level will require more than ten years; all others felt that the speed of his advancement will be consistent with that of his peers and with the expectations the company maintains for college hires. Everyone agreed that he presently displays the abilities and potential to perform effectively at the district level. There was disagreement, however, on the question of whether he should be considered a candidate for above-district positions. Approximately half of the staff felt that his nervousness and tendency to depend a great deal upon superiors argue against his advancing beyond the district level. The other half of the staff predicted that these two characteristics will diminish as he matures and that his general abilities, verbal facility, organizational skills and affable manner will result in his dealing with division level responsibilities successfully.

4

WHAT THEY WERE LIKE

With one exception, the six assessment centers set up in five successive summers to evaluate Management Progress Study subjects for the first time were located in metropolitan hotels. To these locations, with varying degrees of willingness, traveled the 274 college graduate management recruits, the subjects of this book. Few, if any, realized that they were about to become involved in an activity that would seek their cooperation for many years.

The first hour of each Monday afternoon was devoted to an explanation by the Director of why the participants were there and what the Study was all about. This session afforded the first opportunity to see what manner of men Bell System recruiters had gathered to fill the management needs of the future.

Casual initial observation certainly did not support the then faddish notion of the "organization man." The recruits obviously came in all shapes and sizes. Some were seemingly mature and self-confident; others were painfully young and ill at ease. Some were friendly and pleasantly stimulated by the unusual situation; a few were sullen or otherwise hostile. On these and many other dimensions, the recruits were a highly assorted group. Bell System selection methods had clearly not followed any stereotype. The psychologists on the assessment staff wondered, however, whether there was not more homogeneity underneath, yet to be revealed by the assessment center measurements.

The recruits did in fact span a decade in age, the youngest being 21 and the oldest 31. All but a few, however, were within the 22–27 range. They had been born and brought up in many different states, a circumstance guaranteed by the geographic distribution of the telephone companies involved. The Pacific Coast and the Deep South regions were hardly represented, however, in the group.

The rather wide variation in age occurred mainly because military service had intervened between college graduation and Bell System employment or had come up immediately after System employment. (It was the practice at that time to employ promising candidates even though military service was imminent. Some Study subjects were just starting their telephone careers even though, strictly speaking, they had become employees several years previously.) Forty-five percent were veterans. Another 11 percent were in the active Reserve. Thirty-eight percent of those with military experience held, or had held, commissions.

Telephone company employment was not the first full-time job for all in the sample—approximately 30 percent had worked elsewhere. Some had undertaken a post-high school job before deciding to attend college or to help raise funds to attend college. A few had interrupted their college educations to work. Others had accepted what they had thought would be permanent positions following graduation from college but had left for one reason or another. A considerable work history was, however, the exception; fewer than one out of ten of the recruits had had more than a year of full-time experience.

As might be expected from the information just presented, a good many of the recruits were married, and more than a few were fathers. The modal state—44 percent of the sample—was to be single; 25 percent were married but childless, and 21 percent were married with one child. One man was already the father of five! (The reader may have begun to hypothesize that some of the foregoing biographical data would correlate with performance of Bell System employment. For example, would not married men be less likely to leave? These relationships are tested in a later chapter.

For the present, the aim is merely to describe the group of management recruits.)

Nearly all the men in the sample (90 percent) had terminated their formal education with the bachelor's degree. Only 3 percent had a graduate degree, and an additional 7 percent had had some graduate work. Bell System college employment has always been roughly equally open to technical, business, and liberal arts graduates, and the Management Progress Study group reflects this policy. Thirty-five percent had majored in social science or the humanities, an equal number in business administration, and the remaining 30 percent in science and engineering. The science and engineering men, incidentally, had undertaken graduate work far less frequently than men in the other two types of major. Data on educational attainment are summarized in Table 4.*

THEIR EXPECTATIONS

Particularly striking things were the management recruits' extremely favorable expectations of what life in the Bell System would be like. Optimism was apparent in the interviews conducted at the assessment center, in informal conversations, and in answers to essay

Table 4   Educational Attainment

	Social Science and Humanities	Science and Engineering	Business Administration	Total
Bachelor's degree	86	75	84	245
Graduate work	10	2	6	18
Graduate degree	2	2	4	8
Total	98	79	94	271

* Three men who died during the first eight years of the Study are excluded from this and other tables.

questions about their views of the future. It was most explicitly evident in their answers to a questionnaire called the Expectations Inventory.

The Expectations Inventory contained 56 statements describing the situation in which a recruit might find himself at some point in the future.* One statement, for example, was "I live in a desirable community with relatively easy access to my job." The subject was instructed to read each statement and respond to it as he thought he would respond five years in the future. After he had done this, he was supposed to go back over the statements and mark the five which he most wanted to turn out to be true and the five which he most hoped would not come true.

One way of judging the favorableness of the expectations so recorded is to examine the statements that were deemed most important by the recruits. There were seven such statements marked as having great positive importance by more than a third of the subjects. Three of these concerned job challenge and opportunity; not only were they deemed important, but nearly all the subjects expected them to prove true:

	Percentage with Favorable Expectations
My job is challenging with many opporties to learn and do new things.	98
I have a real chance to follow my basic interests and work at the things I like to do.	95
I am advanced about as rapidly as my interest and ability warrant.	88

Two of the items held to be important by the subjects concerned interpersonal satisfactions of a social nature. These were almost unanimously expected to materialize:

I have discovered that working for the
Bell System has helped me to meet the

* The Expectations Inventory was constructed by Elliot G. Mishler and Douglas W. Bray.

kind of people I like and to engage in
desirable social and community activities.   99

My wife is happy that I work for the
Bell System.   99

The other two highly important items concerned pay and promotion. Although a clear majority expected a favorable outcome, expectations were less favorable than for the foregoing items. This is because one's own ability enters into these expectations, and some individuals apparently had doubts:

I am earning $8000 a year or more.   80

I have reached the district level of responsibility. (The district level is the third of seven levels of management running from foreman to president.)   61

Five statements were agreed on by more than one-third of the recruits as being very important negatively; that is they wished strongly that the statements would not prove to be true. One of these items was in the job challenge area, and once again expectations were highly favorable. Only 5 percent expected the worst to happen:

The company doesn't provide sufficient opportunity for me to learn new things.   5

Two items on the negative side concerned promotion:

I have fewer opportunities for promotion than if I had gone to work for a different company.   13

I have not reached as high a level of responsibility as most of the men who started in the company when I did.   20

One item was again directed at the family:

I feel an increasing amount of conflict between obligations of my job and my family.   10

The final item selected as having great negative importance was a global and flat-footed statement, and one that naturally would not be expected by very many who had just made a job choice:

> I regret not having gone to work for
> another company.   I

The extreme favorability of expectations is revealed also by the correlation between the importance of the items as judged by the subjects and their expectations about them. When the 56 items were ranked on importance and again by expectation and a rank correlation computed, the resulting coefficient was .87—very close agreement. What the recruits wanted, they expected to get, and what they did not want was expected to remain only an unpleasant possibility.

The great optimism of the recruits struck the assessment staff, most of whom were considerably older, as highly unrealistic. Yet favorable expectations could hardly be otherwise. Few of the subjects had worked for any large corporation, particularly as a management trainee. Most of them had also considered several other job offers, yet they had selected the Bell System as their employer. Their knowledge of the Bell System came mostly from the individuals who had interviewed them for employment.

Favorable expectations were the product also of a lack of self-knowledge on the part of some of the recruits. They had never competed in a business enterprise, but their college and Bell System recruiters, often inadvertently, had enhanced any favorable view they might have had of themselves. Many mentioned that having been accepted by the Bell System was evidence that they had high ability. One of the more colorful recruits put his view of himself this way: "I can beat my way through dead wood any time."

Whatever its source, the recruits' rosy view of the immediate future emphasized that entry into one's career is a critical point in life. It seemed certain that many would experience disappointment with the company for which they had come to work and with themselves. This would be true, of course, even if they had accepted a position elsewhere. How the recruits would react to the shock of reality and how their expectations would change appeared certain to be interesting aspects of the longitudinal study.

THEIR GENERAL INTELLECTUAL QUALITY

Compared with run-of-the-mill college graduates, the management recruits as a group were better than average. Although Bell System rank-in-class guidelines certainly had not been rigorously applied in their selection, 31 percent had been in the top quarter of their respective graduating classes and another 30 percent had been in the next highest quarter; 21 percent were in the next to the lowest quarter, with 18 percent in the lowest quarter. These ranks had been earned in a better-than-average group of colleges. Approximately 100 colleges and universities were involved, and these were classified into quarters according to indices published in *The Younger American Scholar* (Knapp and Greenbaum, 1953). When this was done, 29 percent of the colleges fell into the highest quarter and 32 percent in the next highest quarter, for a total of 61 percent above the median; 25 percent were in the next lowest quarter, and only 14 percent in the lowest quarter.

This college achievement information was supplemented by the scores on the School and College Ability Test,* a mental ability measure administered at the assessment center. The results parallel the rank-in-class data rather closely. Some 62 percent were above the average score earned by college seniors generally, another 29 percent were in the next to the bottom quarter, but only 9 percent were in the lowest quarter. The data on college achievement are summarized in Table 5.

The assessment interviewers began to comment early that the recruits seemed to be woefully uninformed about current events and that it was difficult to carry on a conversation with some of them except on subjects such as sports. These impressions were verified by the results on a test of knowledge of contemporary affairs administered to every subject at the center. This test consisted of 120 items covering national and international affairs,

---

* Cooperative Test Division, Educational Testing Service, Princeton, N.J.

Table 5   College Achievement

	Rank in Graduating Class (%)	Quality of College (%)	Mental Ability Test Score (%)
Top quarter	31	29	28
Third quarter	30	32	34
Second quarter	21	25	29
Lowest quarter	18	14	9
Total	100%	100%	100%

science and medicine, the arts, and hobbies; it was restricted to the events of the calendar year prior to the year in which assessment took place. The recruits' scores were compared with a norm group of a random sample of third level telephone company managers. The results were strikingly poor. Only 6 percent stood in the top quarter, and only 24 percent did better than the average third level man. Forty-nine percent scored in the lowest quarter. These results are seen even more negatively when we consider that many System executives did not consider the norm group itself as particularly well informed.

THEIR MOTIVATION

An obviously important question involves the extent to which the recruits were motivated to achieve in the work environment. Two assessment techniques that were expected to throw light on such motivation were the personal interview and the projective tests. Lengthy narrative reports on both these methods were read and deliberated on by the assessment center staff in considering each recruit, particularly in judging work and career motivation, dependency, and passivity. These interview and projective reports were analyzed more deliberately some years later for research purposes (Grant and Bray, 1969; Grant, Katkovsky, and Bray, 1967) and rated on a number of significant dimensions. Nearly half these ratings were predictive of progress in management at a statistically reliable level. One such variable, Achievement Motivation, was from the projective reports; three others, from the interview reports, were Need Advancement, Primacy of Work, and Energy. These variables were defined as follows:

Achievement Motivation (Projectives). How ambitious, motivated, and interested in advancement and success is he?

Need Advancement (Interview). To what extent will he need to be promoted significantly earlier than his peers in a job? Consider the level he aspires to and the rapidity with which he expects to achieve it.

Primacy of Work (Interview). To what extent will he find satisfactions from work more important than satisfactions from other areas of life? Consider the value he places on work, the satisfactions he obtains from it relative to other satisfactions (e.g., family, hobbies, community activities), and his willingness to devote more than the required time to his job.

Energy (Interview). How continuously can he sustain a high level of work activity? Consider his general activity level, the effort he puts into his work, and his reactions to expending energy (e.g., evidence of fatigue).

Table 6 shows the percentages of recruits who received above average, average, and below average ratings on each of these variables. The group looked just about average on the projective test rating; on the interview ratings, however, the new hires seemed to be definitely high in these variables, which were intended to indicate their ambition and the zeal with which they were expected to attack their jobs.

THEIR DEPENDENCY AND SECURITY NEEDS

Another cluster of qualities that the assessment staff felt would be important in later career success centered around the concepts of

Table 6   Ratings of Some Work Motives

	Achieve-ment Motiva-tion[1] (%)	Need Advance-ment[2] (%)	Primacy of Work[2] (%)	Energy[2] (%)
Above average	37	61	48	60
Average	31	20	31	27
Below average	32	19	21	13
Total	100%	100%	100%	100%

[1] Projective tests.
[2] Interview.

dependency and security needs. Again the projective tests yielded one rating that predicted progress several years later, and the interview yielded three. These variables and their definitions follow:

Dependence (Projectives). To what extent is he described as needing or seeking help, advice, direction, and encouragement from others?

Need Approval of Superiors (Interview). To what extent does he seek approval of persons in authority over him? Consider his dependence on superordinates for help and guidance as well as tendencies to solicit praise and support from them.

Need Approval of Peers (Interview). To what extent does he seek approval of his peers? Consider his dependence on his coordinates for help and guidance as well as tendencies to solicit support from them.

Need Security (Interview). To what extent does this man need a secure job (not necessarily with the Bell System)? Consider his motives in accepting a position in the Bell System, his views about leaving the System, and his view regarding alternative employment.

Table 7   Ratings of Some Dependency Motives

	Depend-ence[1] (%)	Need Approval— Superiors[2] (%)	Need Approval— Peers[2] (%)	Need Security[2] (%)
Above average	40	80	67	60
Average	25	7	16	13
Below average	35	13	17	27
Total	100%	100%	100%	100%

[1] Projective tests.
[2] Interview.

Table 7 gives the percentages of recruits who received above average, average, and below average ratings on these variables. Once again, the findings are more pronounced for the interview variables, according to which this group of young men appeared to be quite dependent, definitely interested in job security, and eager for support from their bosses and their peers.

THEIR MANAGEMENT POTENTIAL

It will be recalled that the young men were selected by college recruiters and accepted by operating departments on the conviction that they had potential to reach at least the third level of management within ten years of the time of employment. Nearly every recruit expected the same thing; more than half of them, in fact, said they expected to reach such a level in five years. Thus one very important question was the validity of such expectations.

When the Management Progress Study assessment staffs had heard all the reports detailing the behavior at the assessment center of each recruit and had rated each one on 25 presumed managerial qualities, they concluded by stating whether they expected the individuals to reach third level management in ten years' time. Table 8 shows the results. The staff felt sure that nearly half

Table 8   Assessment Staff Prediction
of Reaching Third Level Management
in Ten Years

Prediction	Percentage
Yes	40
Questionable	12
No	48
Total	100%

(48 percent) would not experience such early success but were unable to reach consensus on 12 percent. In 40 percent of the cases, early success *was* predicted.

A SUMMARY VIEW

What were they like, then, this group of young men who had chosen to make the telephone business their life work? A summary would be as follows. Although not a superior group, they were a better-than-average sample of America's college graduates in terms of general mental ability. Their abilities had not been channeled into intellectual activities, however, nor were they well informed or broadly interesting people. They fitted to some extent the popular stereotype of the young "business type" as being eager to get ahead, willing to work hard, yet interested in security and not very independent. They looked to the future with highly favorable expectations—the company would be a fine place to work, and they would succeed in it.

It took no great prophet to foresee what was going to happen. The Bell System, like all human institutions, is imperfect. Not all assignments would be challenging, some supervisors would be less than stimulating leaders, incompetence would sometimes go un-noticed, and some virtue would be ignored. And even were the System perfect, disappointment loomed inevitably. Some recruits were quite mistaken about their own abilities and about even their own motivation. Reality lay ahead.

What would happen as youthful inexperience gave way to the realities of the adult world of work? How many would chuck it and try to do better elsewhere? Would they be the more or the less capable and motivated? Would the "failures" blame the company or themselves? How would early success affect the lucky ones? What would happen to the abilities, motivation, and values of the recruits as they grew older in the corporate environment? Which few will become the top executives of the 1980s? The longitudinal study to come hoped to shed some light on these and numerous other questions.

5

TRACKING THE RECRUITS

When the recruits left the assessment center and returned to their jobs, they fanned out geographically into many cities spread through 20 states. They were further dispersed by being assigned to one of the several departments that make up a telephone company. Some were in headquarters staff assignments and others were in line operations. Keeping track of the details of their experiences and their reactions to them promised to be a formidable task.

The Study design, as shown in Chapter 1, called for every recruit to be intensively interviewed each year for the seven years following assessment. In addition, data and opinions about the recruit were to be collected in six of these seven years by interviews with personnel supervisors and with at least three managers who had directly supervised the recruit during this early stage of his career. Had all the recruits remained with the Bell System, more than 4000 interviews would have been needed.

It was considered important that the interviews with the recruits be conducted by trained professionals. Since Bell System psychologists were seldom available for this work, most of the interviewing was done during the summer months by individuals especially employed for this purpose—faculty members and advanced graduate students from various colleges and universities.

Twenty-three of these excellent interviewers traveled back and forth across much of America. Fortunately, several of the best of them were available for more than one summer, and some carried out their important role in the Study for ten or more years.

For the interviews with company management, it was thought best to use experienced Bell System people who would have a good knowledge of company organization and job assignments. This background would enable them to interact knowledgeably with the interviewees and to cut through more quickly to the specifics of the recruit's job and the job setting, including the type of organization and the characteristics of his supervisor and co-workers.

Several of the System telephone companies, particularly those in the Study, made a major contribution to the research by lending a total of 27 middle managers to conduct these "in-company" interviews. To eliminate any possible bias and to ensure confidentiality, no one interviewed in his home company. Like the professionals, each Bell manager had to travel extensively to do his job.

Not all the 4000-plus interviews were undertaken. One recruit resigned from the company less than two months after he was assessed, and many more followed—either voluntarily or because the company had given up on them. In all, about 100 were gone before eight years had elapsed. Although, as will be seen, they were not lost to the Study, they were not interviewed as frequently as those who stayed, and "in-company" interviews were no longer needed. Nevertheless, 2768 interviews were conducted in the seven years following the original assessment.

A special word is needed about the terminators. When a recruit resigned from the business or was let go, an effort was made to interview him as soon as possible after he actually left. In addition, those in the company who knew most about him and his reasons for leaving were also queried. The recruit was told during his interview that his continued participation in the Study was most important to the research, and he was informed that further interviews would be requested in the years ahead. The response of these men has been gratifying indeed. They have participated in the follow-up interviewing as cooperatively as those who stayed with the Bell System.

As time passed, the number of terminators grew, and the former Bell System men spread out to the four corners of the United States as well as to other parts of the world. Reasons of economy dictated that they could no longer be visited and interviewed face to face. As a compromise, a telephone interview was tried with great success. A preliminary letter prepared the individuals for the interviewer's call, and conversations lasting an hour were not uncommon.

The follow-up interviews with the recruits who remained with the System were conducted in the interviewer's hotel or motel room and were scheduled at a rate of only two a day. Thus the session could be as lengthy as necessary, and the interviewer had an opportunity to dictate his report on each man while the material was fresh. Interviewers took extensive notes, and the resulting reports often filled a dozen single-spaced pages. Excerpts from a few of these reports reveal the high degree of detail that could be captured, as well as the rapport established.

One man told us how he had made some changes in an office:

> The order production center I was in charge of had 29 people in it when I took over, and when I gave it back to the district in April it had 39. This is essentially a production job. These people take the orders that have been written up by the Service Reps, retype them, and put them on tape. The tape is then used to pulse the information to the various departments, such as Accounting, Plant, Directory, etc. We had some real problems in this particular group. There were some real peak periods of work, and we had to build the force up quite a bit. When I first took over, the people were accustomed to shifting positions at will. A girl might be typing today and checking tomorrow. This tends to hurt production because the typing end of the deal is the most critical and the best way of running the organization is to have your best typists typing all the time. Therefore when I went into the organization, I stopped this shifting

around. This had two effects. It not only improved the efficiency of the organization but it also increased my ability to determine accountability. It's a lot easier now to see who is making the errors.

Another man had done a lot of thinking about promotion:

This telephone company is ultraconservative about advancement. I feel I'll need a total of ten years service in order to make third level. I feel my progress is satisfactory, nevertheless. I have a lot to lose, however, if our index goes back to its old level. If it goes well, I think I will have a good chance to make third level. I'm now 33 and possibly I'm getting too old to expect to ever make fifth level. I figure I should make third level at about age 35, and fourth level at about 40. I haven't been looking for any other jobs, and I'm satisfied with the work I'm doing. If I stay at second level the rest of my life, I think I would be satisfied as long as the work I was doing was agreeable to me.

A discussion of activities outside work revealed that one recruit, at least, was not very interested in them:

He belongs to a Protestant church and to the Masons. He also belongs to a mechanical engineers' society which he describes as something you belong to but don't participate much in, if at all. He rarely goes to the movies, perhaps once a year. He doesn't watch T.V. at all in the summer since he's busy with other things. In the winter when they're sort of snowbound, he and his wife watch it a few hours an evening. He says he reads extremely little, especially books, but he does read **Time, Reader's Digest,** and a couple of sporting magazines. He looks at the local paper every day. He has invested money in the stock market but does not have much interest in it. A friend takes care of it; the investments are good solid stocks. He belongs to no civic organizations.

Another recruit was very pleased with his supervisor:

> I think my boss is the best third level man in the telephone
> company. He's all man and he's completely fair, he plays
> no favorites. One of his weak points might be his lack of
> organization. He's still an engineer at heart rather than an
> executive and he wants to keep his fingers on the details.
> He's slow to make decisions. As far as my rating is con-
> cerned, I really don't know. He says I'm doing a good job,
> but he's too busy to give individual personnel reviews. I
> heard, however, that I got one of the two highest ratings
> in the department. Apart from these things, I would say he's
> a great person who goes to bat for his men.

The interviews with management personnel to whom the recruits
reported, or had reported, were somewhat more variable than
those with the recruits themselves. Some managers were not
particularly good observers of those who worked for them (an
important fact in its own right); a few were more interested in
talking about their own problems than reporting on a subordinate.
For the most part, however, these interviews were very important
and revealing encounters. The following lengthy excerpt is taken
from the discussion with a district manager about a recruit who
had reported to him for about two years, dating from the start
of the third year the recruit was employed by the company. The
recruit had clearly impressed this manager with his ability to get
results in spite of some disturbing aspects of his interpersonal
behavior.

> This man was very successful in performing his job. His
> results were very good and consistently at or above the
> target level. He wanted to be the best and worked very
> hard at it. He displayed great initiative. He is, however,
> highly self-motivated, overly ambitious and aggressive, and
> has no apparent deep feelings for people. He seemed to
> treat them only as a means to get where he wanted to go.
> He displayed a very superior attitude and seemed to take
> delight in placing others in a bad light.

His appraisals were outstanding based on his high job performance and ability to get good results. He is a very intelligent person who accepts responsibility well and works very hard. He has high standards. He is calm under pressure; in fact, he seems to thrive on it. He does have difficulty in admitting to being wrong and he tries to talk his way out of trouble.

He finds it difficult to tolerate opposition to his views. He is usually right, but he is so tactless and forceful in expressing his opinion that others resent it. Status and money are very important to him. He does not have a very good sense of humor and he also seems to lack a sense of loyalty.

An interview with the boss of another man suggests a much more pedestrian recruit:

I have no complaints at all with the work that he turns in. He is a very good stable employee. He does a fine job for the company and his feeling for the company and its policies is a good one. He is not a world-beater but he will do a good job. He is extremely cooperative, a nice guy to have around. He hasn't exhibited any weak points to me, but, aside from his ability to catch on to work that is completely foreign to him, he has shown no other real noticeable strong points.

Sometimes bosses were a little more talkative than the interviewer bargained for. At the end of twelve single-spaced pages, one weary reporter confessed, "Well, the interview went on for three hours and I think I have a better story on the boss interviewed than on the man I was supposed to be getting information on." Any complaints, however, would be definitely ungrateful. The cooperation of hundreds of Bell System managers in providing information to an interviewer they had just met and for a study some of them knew little about was remarkable.

When a recruit left the Bell System, an attempt was made to conduct a special "exit" interview with him as soon as possible.

Sometimes more time elapsed than anticipated; one man, for example, was on his way to a job in Spain by the time his resignation was reported. In most cases, however, it was possible to talk to the terminator within a few weeks of the time he left. Once again, cooperation was noteworthy. Everyone who left was interviewed, and all but a few have continued to provide information even after years away from System employment.

Since termination of management recruits represents a significant cost to a business as well as often being painful to the recruit himself, an entire chapter is devoted to the information obtained from the exit interviews. The nature of these interviews is only suggested at this point. One man, for example, had multiple reasons for calling it a day, as these excerpts from his interview indicate:

> One day the recruit walked into his boss's office quite confident that he'd completed a good job and expecting to be complimented. Instead the roof fell in. He was told that he was arrogant, had an antagonistic attitude, and just wanted to argue, not to be helped. . . . The recruit hated the city he had to work in and had assumed when he took the job that he would be given a transfer. He made attempts to get such a transfer, but they were not successful. . . . He was involved in a love affair and wanted to work nearer the young woman. . . . He also had a strong desire to return to school.

Another man who left after short service seemed to be motivated more by temperamental incompatibility with the telephone company than by practical concerns. The psychologist who interviewed him summarized his impression as follows:

> My general impression is that this man is an active, somewhat impulsive person who is attracted to change, excitement, and masculine activities. These characteristics, together with his rejection of job security and dislike of routine, probably constitute the chief reasons for his decid-

ing to leave the company. His decisions about his future job choices will probably be dictated to a large extent by the immediate situation in which he is involved. He is not the sort of person who makes careful plans or analyzes all possibilities; he seems to prefer fast action. He is not very achievement oriented. He is likely to exhibit drive and assertiveness, but I think these characteristics are associated more with his direct, masculine approach to life than with the desire to achieve. He is not interested in status and his job goals are associated with gaining pleasure from excitement and change rather than with monetary rewards.

The design of the Management Progress Study called for the management recruits to go through an assessment center at the start of their careers and then again eight years later. These two thorough evaluations of the men were intended to yield measurements of change in abilities and other personal characteristics over the early years of a career in business management. To understand these changes, however, it was necessary to obtain as detailed a picture as possible of each man's experiences during the intervening years. It was deemed to be particularly important to know the specific duties of the several jobs each man was assigned during this period, the type and extent of training he received, the kinds of supervisors he had, how they and others reacted to him, and what feedback, if any, he received about his performance and his future. Clearly, moreover, it seemed more advisable to learn the recruit's reaction to all these conditions on an annual basis than to depend on his retrospection of the eight years at the second assessment center.

It was to provide such information that interviews such as those quoted from in this chapter were conducted. More than 20,000 pages of typescript resulted, providing not only a wealth of the desired detail but also a formidable task for analysis and summary.

6

COMPANY ENVIRONMENT
AND EARLY CAREERS

When the recruits joined the Bell System in the latter half of the 1950s, they became part of a very large business organization— they had more than 700,000 fellow employees. The basic part of this business, referred to humorously by some of the staff as POTS (plain old telephone service), included 58 million telephones— 82 percent of the instruments in use in the United States. Investment in plant and equipment totaled 21 billion dollars. Almost 2 million shareholders owned stock in the business.

Not only was the organization large, it was still growing rapidly. By the end of the 1960s, more than 90 million telephones were in use, and investment in plant and equipment was 47 billion dollars. Employees numbered just under a million.

The Bell System is made up of a number of different organizations, under the parent company, American Telephone & Telegraph. The Western Electric Company is the manufacturing and supply arm; Bell Telephone Laboratories are responsible for basic research and development of new equipment and methods. The Long Lines Department of AT&T provides long distance telephone service. Finally, there are the telephone companies themselves, which provide service in each of the 48 continental states. At the start of the Study there were 19 such companies, each with its own president and board of directors.

The men in the Management Progress Study were initially employed by one of the following telephone companies—Chesapeake and Potomac, Michigan, Mountain, Northwestern, and Pennsylvania. These companies varied both in the size of organization, although none could be considered small, and in area serviced. Pennsylvania, although not large in territory, was the biggest company; Mountain and Northwestern covered between them the vast area from Idaho and the Dakotas south to the Mexican border.

Each telephone company is organized along both geographical and functional lines. At the outset of the Study, Michigan Bell was a single area company—the state of Michigan. Northwestern Bell had five state areas—Iowa, Minnesota, Nebraska, North Dakota, and South Dakota. Mountain consisted of eight areas—Idaho, Montana, Wyoming, Utah, Colorado, Arizona, New Mexico, and West Texas. Pennsylvania was divided into three operating areas in the state and included, through a separate board of directors, the Diamond State Company (covering the state of Delaware). Chesapeake and Potomac actually consisted of four companies— Maryland, Virginia, West Virginia, and the District of Columbia— each with its own headquarters.

Telephone companies are organized functionally into departments, the major ones (described later) being Plant, Traffic, Commercial, Accounting, and Engineering. These departments are divided geographically into divisions, which are further subdivided into districts. The resulting districts vary greatly in area, depending on the concentration of demand for telephone service. A district in a sparsely settled area may cover several hundred square miles; one covers "only" the tip of Manhattan island.

Management structure within departments follows the typical pyramid pattern. The top position is Department Head, which is five levels up from the lowest management level. The Division Head is fourth level, and the District Manager is third level—the bottom rung of middle management. It is this "district level" which the college recruits in the Study were supposed to be able to reach within five to ten years of employment.

INITIAL PLACEMENT

The recruit's early experiences as a manager varied considerably depending on the telephone company he joined and the department to which he was assigned. The latter factor was particularly important in the life of the recruit, since it influenced such matters as nature of the work, opportunity for advancement, and area of telephone operations in which he would become expert.

More than four-fifths of the recruits were assigned to one of four departments—Plant, Traffic, Commercial, and Engineering; 12 percent were assigned to Accounting, with the remainder (5 percent) going to the other departments. As a rule, the assignment of individuals to departments was incorporated into the employment process; that is assignments were made before the recruit actually joined the company. In the one company that did things differently, assignment to a department was made following 42 weeks of initial training. The individual's preferences were always considered in making departmental assignments, but company needs and the impression made by the recruit were controlling.

In spite of the similarities between the groups of men assigned to each of the departments, there were wide differences among the departments in the general management potential of the recruits they selected. When the recruits were evaluated at the Management Progress Study assessment center soon after employment, 40 percent of the total group were judged to have middle management potential. Those assigned to the Traffic Department, however, showed a corresponding figure of 71 percent. At the other extreme, only 21 percent of those assigned to Engineering were rated as well. It appears that Engineering weighted technical knowledge more heavily than general managerial characteristics in selecting its men; perhaps, too, it was impossible to find enough recruits who had the needed educational background and also high managerial potential. Of the men assigned to Plant, one-third of whom were technical graduates, 42 percent were assessed as having middle management potential.

ORIENTATION AND TRAINING

Although there were common threads in the orientation and training of the recruits, specific programs varied from location to location. Initial orientation was usually conducted by a middle manager from Personnel or from the recruit's department, or by a training supervisor. The orientation process involved a combination of interviews, formal sessions, and on-the-job discussions. In some locations the recruit was given specific information about the company's expectations regarding his performance and progress (e.g., "He should demonstrate potential for middle management during the first year or be asked to leave.").

Most of the training programs were extensive; some lasted as long as two years. There was strong emphasis on learning the basics of telephone operations, at least within the individual's department. The programs, therefore, usually required that the recruit actually work in a number of nonmanagement assignments. Some of these rotational assignments lasted several months. Another ubiquitous aspect of the training programs was exposure to the work of the other departments. This was usually accomplished by lecture techniques and extensive reading assignments, although actual rotation into other departments was far from unknown. Last, but not least in importance, management development courses were offered. A few of the more promising recruits were given the opportunity to attend development courses offered by universities as well as the in-house programs.

Methods used for evaluating the performance of the new trainees varied from company to company. In the typical case, the recruit was evaluated semiannually by his supervisor. These evaluations were usually reviewed by higher level line or personnel managers. In some cases the recruit was given feedback about his performance and apparent potential; in others he received little or no information.

Salary programs for the recruits were similar in all locations. Each provided for differing start rates depending on background factors such as college major (technical graduates usually received a higher starting salary), advanced degrees, previous work experience, and military service. Salary progression programs, however, were quite rigid as long as one stayed in the status of trainee. Increases of about the same percentage were given at predetermined intervals as long as an individual was doing passably well or better. A trainee could expect to be receiving about 15 percent more than his starting salary 18 to 24 months after beginning to work.

Once the recruit left the status of trainee, he went on the regular salary plan for all management employees. This usually required a qualitative rating of the manager's job performance and a resulting determination of the percentage increase to be given and the time at which it would be given. Intervals might vary from 12 to 18 months or longer, and the percentage from 8 to 15 percent, depending on merit.

It cannot be said that the recruits viewed their training experiences with uniform enthusiasm. The annual interviews with the men conducted as part of the Study elicited many complaints. Some said that their training had been unceremoniously interrupted, or even terminated, by operating demands or by the recession of 1958. Another weakness, the trainees said, was that the value of some of the training assignments depended heavily on the interest of the supervisor one happened to draw, and some were not very interested. Many reported that they had not been given all the feedback they felt they should have on their performance and on how their potential was evaluated. (As a result of these findings, early training programs for high-potential college recruits were drastically revised throughout the Bell System.)

ON THE JOB

When a recruit left trainee status, he became a member of lower level management (although he was not necessarily supervising others). His career target was normally expected to be a third level management position in his department—the job of District Manager. Although the actual details of a third level job may vary considerably even within the same department, each trainee had at least a vague idea of the kind of responsibilities that lay in his future if he moved along as expected.

The Plant Department is responsible for installing and maintaining communications equipment. A District Plant Manager in a major city might be responsible for servicing 152,000 telephone "stations," including both business and residential customers. Such service, and new installation work, includes manual switchboards, automatic call distributors, data services, and teletype. The District Manager would be responsible also for equipment such as toll switching machines. His force would number 400, including 50 first and second level supervisors.

The Engineering Department plans and makes arrangements for the construction of the telephone "plant," including buildings as well as telephone equipment such as that just described. A District Engineer (Switching) for example, might be responsible for providing engineering services related to all local and long distance switching equipment for an entire state. This would involve forecasting, determining the equipment needed, ordering, and following through the installation of complex switching systems. Annual expenditures for this work might total 20 million dollars, but the organization would be relatively small—about 25 people, nearly all of management level.

The Traffic Department handles telephone calls and determines the quantity and arrangement of circuits and associated facilities necessary. A typical District Traffic Manager is responsible for supervising and directing forecasting, planning, administrative operations, and end results connected with operator services. He might be responsible for the amount and quality of service rendered by toll and directory assistance operators in six central offices servicing 200,000 stations. A major concern would be the provision of adequate forces to handle traffic volumes in an economical and efficient manner. His work force might total 750, and at least 700 of these would be nonmanagement and union-represented employees.

The Commercial Department handles business relations with telephone company customers. A District Commercial Manager typically manages a force that acts as the main contact point between the company and the public with regard to establishing, modifying, and discontinuing telephone service. His organization is also responsible for collection of accounts, and it handles a wide variety of customer complaints and questions regarding billing and service. Collection activities may total several million dollars per month. The manager represents the company to the public and may be regarded as "Mr. Telephone" in the community. His organization, which might serve 100,000 residence and 20,000 business accounts, might number 130.

The Accounting Department has two main functions—recording and collecting all revenues earned by the company (revenue accounting), and recording and paying out all monies owed to the company's suppliers and employees (disbursement accounting). One District Accounting Manager is responsible for processing all service orders originated for accounts in one area of a heavily populated state. This requires generation of computer input media used for computerized billing of local service, message unit, toll, and directory advertising charges. The billing includes both residence and business accounts (PBX, Centrex, utilities, national accounts, and directory advertising). The work must be completed within fixed time frames, to accomplish scheduled release of bills. The manager is also responsible for conducting special studies to assure accuracy of billing and for generating various company statistics and reports. The district is responsible for 700,000 customer accounts, including 3,600 PBX and 28 Centrex accounts. The District Manager has a force of 178, including 155 union-represented clerks.

This brief overview indicates the typical jobs that most of the recruits could see in the future. Some, of course, had aspirations for eventually finding their way into "nonoperating" assignments, such as personnel or public relations, but these jobs very rarely lay in their direct path. Most were being primed by the company for a District job in the department they were then in, and this is what most recruits hoped to attain.

ON THE MOVE

By the end of eight years, the point at which they were reassessed, the original group of 274 recruits had dropped to 167 still in the employ of the System. Three, unfortunately, were dead, and 104 had found employment elsewhere. Those who left form the basis of Chapter 11; the early careers of those who remained at least until reassessment are considered here.

Reassessment found nearly all the men (91 percent) who were still with the System on duty with their original telephone company. A few of them had been elsewhere—usually to the AT&T, the parent company—during the eight years, but had returned. Fewer than 10 percent were not with their "home" company at reassessment; most of these were with AT&T, a very few were with other System companies. This lack of appreciable intercompany mobility is the rule for Bell System management below the third level of management; even when that level is reached, most of the movement consists of a period of service at AT&T, followed by return to the original company. Movement between the telephone companies is rare until one becomes an officer.

Within each telephone company, however, there was much mobility between departments. More than half the recruits (57 percent) had changed departments at least once. One man had been in five departments! These shifts of department, it should be noted, seldom were made with the purpose of providing developmental opportunities for the recruit through job rotation. They usually took place because of the needs of the business or, occasionally, because the recruit was not "making it" in one department and it was thought he might be more successful elsewhere. Changes of job within a department, however, were often made for the purpose of development. The plan was that a recruit would develop and prove himself in one department. An interdepartmental move for further development was thought to be appropriate after the third level of management was reached.

The extensive interdepartmental movement that nevertheless took place changed the departmental distribution of the recruits from original assessment to reassessment. The percentage of men in Accounting had doubled, going from 12 to 25 percent. The percentage of those who were not in the major departments had risen from 5 to 12 percent, which should not be surprising when it is realized that staff departments such as Personnel and Public Relations obtain much of their people from the operating departments rather than by direct hire. The major operating departments—Plant, Traffic, and Commercial—had a smaller percentage of the recruits than they had acquired originally.

The Bell System intent, as previously mentioned, was that college recruits of the vintage of the men in the Study would reach the third (District) level of management within ten years of the time of employment. This goal was almost in the class of a company dogma, even though much evidence existed that it had been approximated. A retrospective statistical study done in the late 1950s showed that after 20 years only 42 percent of the college graduates still on the payroll had reached third level. Viewed against this background, the recruits in the Study had, on the average, progressed just about normally. At the time of reassessment, 37 percent of them were at or above the third level of management.

Progress into middle management differed sharply among the five companies in the Study. Three of them did not depart too far from the average of 37 percent. In one, however, 75 percent of those reassessed were in middle management, and at the other extreme was a company in which only 4 percent had "succeeded"! These discrepancies were due to several factors, including differences in the accuracy of management manpower planning, differences in the degree of potential possessed by the recruits themselves, and the adoption of a new college employment and initial development program that tended to "date" the Management Progress Study recruits.

Progress into middle management varied not only by company but also by the department to which the recruit was originally assigned. Table 9 shows for each department the percentage at or above third level at the time of reassessment. This percentage appears against the base of those still with the company at reassessment (last column) and against the total number originally hired

Table 9   Termination and Progress by Department at Hire

| Original Department | Number of Recruits | | Per-centage Termi-nated | Percentage Promoted to Middle Management | |
	Original Group	Remainder Group		Original Group	Remainder Group
Plant	62	32	48	15	28
Commercial	58	32	45	26	47
Traffic	51	32	37	26	41
Engineering	55	46	16	20	24
Accounting	33	24	27	36	50
Other	12	1	92	8	100
Total	271	167	38%	23%	37%

(fourth column). The percentage of those who started in each department but terminated is also given.

Table 9 reveals that progress was greatest in Accounting, whether as a percentage of either the original or the remainder group. Plant and Engineering both showed slow progress, but there is a difference between them. Very few of the recruits (only 16 percent) who started in Engineering had terminated. This would tend to produce more competition for advancement. In Plant, on the other hand, terminations were high (48 percent), yet progress was still slow. Of the dozen men who had started with one of the "other" departments, nearly all had left. The one who remained had reached the third level.

We might ask whether those who moved around during these first eight years forged ahead any more quickly than those who stayed where they had started. The answer is that there was a small but insignificant difference. Thirty-three percent of those who never left their starting department had reached third level by the time of reassessment, as compared with 39 percent of those who had changed departments or served with another unit of the Bell System.

These findings suggest that a recruit's progress is strongly influenced by the organizational setting to which he is originally assigned. Both the particular telephone company he started with and the department in which he went to work influenced his future status. The role of the recruit's own managerial abilities as they interacted with the organizational setting is examined in a later chapter.

Even though progress in management during the first eight years was not all the recruits might have hoped for, they did well when it came to their pay. Median salary more than doubled in the eight years. One recruit tripled his earnings. As might be expected, salary range increased moderately. At the time of original assessment, the least well paid recruit was making 80 percent of the median salary; the best paid made 152 percent. At reassessment the least well paid made 68 percent of the median salary at that time; the best paid man stood at 161 percent of the same figure.

CHANGES IN PERSONAL LIVES

By the time of reassessment much had happened in the personal lives of the recruits. The bulk of the recruits were now 30 to 35 years old, the period sometimes characterized as the "mid-thirties depression." There were substantial changes in their family situations. The modal state (95 percent) was now married, rather than single. Ninety percent were fathers, and more than one-third had three or more children. Although the average salary had more than doubled over the eight-year period, this was a time of home building for most men. Most of the men were in satisfactory financial condition, but many still reported concern over financial matters.

The educational status of the recruits showed little change over the eight-year period. Although only six had earned a graduate degree, approximately 15 percent had taken some additional course work. Naturally, the men had been exposed to System training courses, and it was a rare individual who did not have at least some off-the-job management development activity. In addition, a number of men attended special schools for advanced technical training.

More of the men were veterans, since some had been on leave from the company for service in the post-Korean conflict period. By the time of reassessment, much had changed in the world around them. The major conflict was now in Vietnam, and the subjects themselves were labeled by the writers of the 1960s as the "silent generation." They had passed from the role of management trainee to being managers, some at rather high levels of responsibility. Societal changes had added challenges to the basic one of learning to be capable managers. Disadvantaged people were being added to the System work force in much larger numbers than ever before, and some of these young managers had to deal directly with racial issues on the job as well as at home. Many were now looking across the "generation gap" from the other side as they supervised new recruits from the college classes of the 1960s.

The men in the Study had seen many changes during the brief span of eight years. One of the most important, more immediate changes was the extensive experience that the individual had acquired in the world of work. Some had found that experience challenging and rewarding; more had discovered that reality had not borne out their rosy expectations. What kind of man had been successful? Why had some already reached their zenith only one-fifth of the way into a 40-year career? Most important for the purposes of the Study, what had these eight years of life done to the abilities, personalities, and values of the recruits?

7

DETERMINANTS OF
PROGRESS

Moving upward in the management hierarchy represents a very important fact of life for management recruits. A central concern of the Management Progress Study, therefore, was to discover the factors that led to or hindered advancement. Such knowledge would not only contribute to understanding the lives of the recruits, it would be of great potential value to organizations in improving methods of selecting future recruits and supplying the optimal conditions for their growth and development.

Very broadly, progress in an organization can be conceived of as a product of the characteristics of the employee as these interact with opportunities provided by the organization. The employee's characteristics include his abilities and knowledge, his motivation, and his impact on others. Opportunity involves not merely the number of job openings at higher levels, but chances to display ability and to develop, characteristics of supervisors, methods used to determine promotability, and organizational climate.

In the previous chapter we noted the influence on progress of two opportunity factors—the telephone company for which the recruit worked, and the department to which he was assigned. It was seen that each has a definite effect. Before proceeding to other important facets of the work environment, however, we examine the importance of a recruit's own qualities.

PREDICTION FROM ASSESSMENT

Few believe that development and opportunity alone will produce a successful manager. It would be a rare organization indeed that would be willing to hire any college graduate, sight unseen. Some degree of selection is always insisted on. Even so, many executives are decidedly ambivalent about the recruit selection process and are inclined to doubt that it is really possible to predict how far a young man will go, before he is even on the payroll.

A concluding judgment made at the assessment center through which the recruits entered the Study concerned the likelihood that they would reach the middle level of management within ten years. The predictions and management levels actually attained eight years later by those who remained with the company appear in Table 10.*

Table 10   Assessment Predictions and Attainment of Middle Management Eight Years Later

	N	Number Reaching Middle Management	Percentage Reaching Middle Management
Predicted to reach middle management	61	39	64
Predicted to fail to reach middle management	62	20	32
Total	123	59	48%

* Predictions of success were not made during the first (Michigan Bell) assessment center. Therefore, the number of cases in this and other tables is 123 rather than 167, the total number of recruits who were with the System at reassessment.

It can be noted that 64 percent of those who had been seen to have such potential did reach the third level of management in this period of time, as compared with only 32 percent of those not so judged. This means, very simply, that it is possible to improve substantially on the selections made by ordinary college recruiting processes. It also means that personal characteristics displayed on the day of employment are definitely related to later success. When we consider that this result was obtained in spite of the effects of different rates of progress in different telephone companies and different departments, the accuracy of prediction is even more impressive.

JOB CHALLENGE

Different companies and different departments were not the only variations in the work environment which influenced progress. A closer look at the actual job situation in which each recruit found himself is provided by the annual interview conducted with the recruit and with company personnel. The many interviews were studied by two psychologists, who rated the work environment each subject had experienced during his eight years of employment. Ratings were made on some eighteen variables, which were later combined into the following areas: Job Stimulation and Challenge, Degree of Supervisory Responsibilities, Open versus Structured Assignments, Stress of Assignments, Working Alone versus as a Group Member, Morale of the Work Group, Quality of Supervision, and the Degree to which the Supervisor was an Achievement Model. It should be emphasized that the ratings covered the whole eight years of experience; they were not made separately for each position the subject might have held. Table 11, which correlates these aspects of the work situation and progress in management, reveals that there were significant relationships between advancement and all but two of the ratings. The unrelated ratings had to do with whether the subject worked alone or with a group and with the morale of the work group.

Job characteristics and advancement are not independent variables. If a man does well on one job, he improves his chances that

Table 11   Correlations between Aspects of Work
Situation and Management Level at Reassessment

Factor	Correlation Coefficient
Job stimulation and challenge	.44*
Supervisory responsibilities	.34*
Structured versus unstructured assignments	.48*
Objective stress of assignments	.30*
Working alone versus working in groups	−.08
Morale of groups	.08
Supervision from bosses	.37*
Achievement models of bosses	.43*

*Significant at .01 level ($N = 155$).

his next job will be a more demanding one. If he does poorly on a job, the organization will be reluctant to move him to a more difficult assignment. The correlations in Table 11, therefore, do not by themselves prove that challenging assignments develop a man so that he later receives a promotion. Data presented in a later chapter, however, show that job involvement is a function of job challenge. Therefore, it seems likely that the nature of the job has an effect on motivation, which in turn affects job performance, leading management to conclusions about promotability.

The wide gap between the stimulation and opportunity offered by different sequences of assignments of job and bosses can best be appreciated by concrete examples. The following summary covers the early career of a recruit who experienced high job challenge.

Although his very first jobs in the Traffic Department were of a routine engineering nature, he moved quickly through a wide variety of assignments, where he had an opportunity to perform a range of duties normally required of someone with several years experience. He was given considerable supervisory responsibility, beginning late in his first year, when he supervised ten women in a group fraught with severe personnel problems.

By his second year he was promoted to second level as a Traffic Chief, supervising the Chief Operator in all phases of her work. At the same time he had several special assignments in other offices throughout the district.

Late in his second year he was transferred to the Commercial Department as a Unit Manager. With no Commercial background, he was consistently confronted with new learning experiences providing considerable challenge. This assignment was further complicated by problems related to overstaffing, lack of further opportunity for experienced Service Representatives, etc.

During his third year this man spent several months as a staff member of a Personnel Assessment Center, and was then promoted to District Manager. His supervisory responsibility included 60 managers reporting directly or indirectly to him. He was also responsible for several areas not generally part of the job (public relations, independent contracts, rural service problems).

Several unexpected demands presented themselves which increased the challenge of his job. For example, he had to

- establish a new Personnel Records system

- fight a union attempt to organize girls in the business office

- resist pressure from Chamber of Commerce, local radio and service clubs to establish a 150-mile free calling area

- cut off an attempt by City Council and attorneys to levy a franchise tax

This work career to date has involved being supervised by a series of very demanding bosses. They have been, for the most part, creative and decisive, and have believed firmly in developing subordinates through participation in problem solving.

This exciting introduction into a business career stands in sharp contrast to the experiences of a less fortunate recruit:

This man began as an Operations Assistant in the Engineering Department and split his time between Plant Extension and Transmission and Protection. There was little pressure to produce. Nor was he given an opportunity to "take over" for his boss during his first year and had no supervisory responsibilities. His assignments were routine engineering. During his second year he was rotated between several departments, then returned to Engineering, still with no supervisory responsibility.

He was transferred to Marketing as a Sales Engineer during his third year and promoted to second level. While this assignment did involve learning technical aspects of data handling equipment and gaining sales experience, which he found challenging, learning the general elements of his new job posed no problems for him.

His fourth year found him still at second level with no supervisory responsibilities and no change in job duties. His job was to sell data communications to customers throughout the state. His boss never gave him an assignment he felt he would have difficulty handling.

Much of the cause for the lack of challenge in this man's career rests in his bosses. His first boss did everything himself, giving his men very little latitude; he was afraid of "overloading" them. A later boss did nothing to stimulate creativity. "Meeting deadlines" was his conception of a challenging assignment. He would frequently do things for his men rather than forcing them to develop.

To evaluate more fully the relationship of job stimulation and advancement into middle management, four of the ratings in Table 11 (Achievement Models of Bosses, Job Stimulation and Challenge, Supervisory Responsibilities, and Unstructured Assignments) were combined into one set of ratings—Job Challenge. The recruits were then classified into three groups (high, moderate, and low) on this combined rating. Table 12 lists the percentage of recruits in each group who had reached the third level of management by the time of reassessment. There is a strong relationship. Although almost six out of ten of the men who had experienced high job challenge had reached middle management, fewer than one out of ten of those who had had low challenge had done so.

As has been noted previously, job challenge is not independent of the capabilities of a manager. Those who perform well are more likely to receive challenging assignments. This relationship is shown in Table 13. Recruits who were assessed as having middle management potential were likely to experience high job challenge. (Since assessment information was not available to management, of course, recruits could not have been assigned on the basis of assessment results.) Slightly more than half the men with good potential met with high job challenge, and only 10 percent of them had assignments with low challenge. The situation was quite different for the recruits for whom the assessment staff did not predict middle management. They fell into the high, moderate, and low job challenge categories in about equal proportions.

Did job challenge have different effects on the careers of the more capable and the less capable recruits? Table 14 presents the percentages reaching middle management by the time of reassessment of the high- and low-rated recruits by each job challenge classification. There is a strong relationship (within both groups)

Table 12   Relationship of Job Challenge to
Management Level at Reassessment

		District Level or Higher at Reassessment	
Job Challenge	N	N	%
High	64	38	59
Moderate	64	20	31
Low	39	3	8
Total	167	61	37%

Table 13   Relationship of Assessment Prediction to Later Job Challenge

	Predicted to Reach Middle Management		Predicted to Fail to Reach Middle Management	
Job Challenge	N	%	N	%
High	33	54	18	29
Moderate	22	36	24	39
Low	6	10	20	32
Total	61	100%	62	100%

Table 14   Relationship of Assessment Prediction, Job Challenge, and Management Level at Reassessment

	N	Number Reaching Middle Management	Percentage Reaching Middle Management
Predicted to reach middle management			
High job challenge	33	25	76
Moderate job challenge	22	12	55
Low job challenge	6	2	33
Total	61	39	64%
Predicted to fail to reach middle management			
High job challenge	18	11	61
Moderate job challenge	24	8	33
Low job challenge	20	1	5
Total	62	20	32%

between challenge and arriving at middle management. It is noteworthy that the third level was attained by 61 percent of the recruits whom the assessment said would not reach this level, but who had high challenge assignments. Conversely, only one-third of those who looked good at assessment but had low challenge jobs reached the third level.

The extremes of the table reveal the powerful combined effect of job challenge and individual potential. Just over three-quarters of the more promising recruits who had had challenging jobs were in middle management eight years after employment, as compared with only one in 20 of the less promising recruits who were little challenged!

THE IMPORTANCE OF PERSONAL QUALITIES

Since the assessment staff prediction of progress in management was quite accurate, especially when allowance is made for all the unforeseeable situational variables that militated against prediction, it is advisable to dig a little more deeply into the assessment process itself. The assessment staff, as described previously, organized its view of each recruit around 25 variables, each of which was discussed and rated before a final prediction of the man's progress was made. Insight into the degree to which various qualities influenced the final staff prediction can be gained from the correlations between ratings on the 25 variables and staff prediction. These appear in the first column of Table 15. The second column gives the correlations of the variable ratings with progress in management eight years later.

From the first column of figures we can see that nearly all the variables were significantly related to the overall staff judgment. It is also clear that certain obviously managerial variables such as Human Relations Skills, Organizing and Planning, and Decision Making, were perceived as much more important by the staff than Dependency, Readiness to Adopt Company Values, or Social Objectivity.

Such findings rest on an analysis of assessment staff judgments. The next question is whether the weight accorded these factors by

Table 15   Correlations between Assessment Variable Ratings and Overall Assessment Rating and Management Level at Reassessment

Variable	Overall Assessment Rating* ($N = 207$)	Level at Reassessment** ($N = 123$)
Human Relations Skills	.66	.32
Behavior Flexibility	.63	.21
Organizing and Planning	.61	.28
Need for Advancement	.60	.31
Decision Making	.59	.18
Perception of Threshold Social Cues	.59	.17
Personal Impact	.57	.15
Creativity	.57	.25
Oral Communications Skills	.53	.33
Resistance to Stress	.51	.31
Energy	.51	.28
Primacy of Work	.48	.18
Inner Work Standards	.46	.21
Scholastic Aptitude	.46	.19
Range of Interests	.45	.23
Realism of Expectations	.42	.08
Tolerance of Uncertainty	.39	.30
Self-Objectivity	.38	.04
Need for Security	−.32	−.20
Ability to Delay Gratification	−.30	−.19
Need for Approval of Superiors	−.18	−.14
Need for Approval of Peers	−.16	−.17
Bell System Value Orientation	.15	−.02
Goal Flexibility	−.13	−.18
Social Objectivity	.04	.13

*rs .14 or higher significant at .05 level; .18 or higher significant at .01 level.

**rs .18 or higher significant at .05 level; .23 or higher significant at .01 level.

the assessors corresponds to their importance in actual progress in management. The second column of Table 15 shows the correlations of each assessment variable with progress in management. As would be expected, the correlations of the variables with progress are substantially smaller than with staff predictions. Progress, as has been seen, is greatly influenced by opportunity factors. The stronger the influence of opportunity, the less the influence exerted by personal characteristics.

The pattern of correlations, however, is very similar as we move from the relationship of the variables to the staff prediction to their relationship with actual progress. Tested statistically (by transforming the correlation coefficients to z scores and correlating these scores) this similarity was found to be very high (.94). The assessment staff, therefore, was remarkably accurate in the weighting it accorded implicitly to each personal characteristic as a determinant of advancement in management.

The 25 assessment variables obviously are not independent of one another. To refine the analysis, the variable ratings were factor analyzed, and the resulting factors were examined in their relation to the final assessment judgment of likelihood of progression in management. The results (Bray and Grant, 1966) indicate that the charactertistics essential to managerial success can be grouped into seven areas.

Administrative Skills. A high potential manager plans and organizes his work effectively, makes decisions willingly, and makes high quality decisions.

Interpersonal Skills. A high potential manager makes a forceful and likable impression on others, has good oral presentation skills, leads others to perform, and modifies his behavior when necessary to reach a goal.

Intellectual Ability. A high potential manager learns readily and has a wide range of interests.

Stability of Performance. A high potential manager maintains effective work performance under uncertain or unstructured conditions and in the face of stress.

Work Motivation. A high potential manager finds satisfaction from work more important than those from other areas of life and wants to do a good job for its own sake.

Career Orientation. A high potential manager wants to advance significantly more rapidly than his peers, is **not** as concerned as others about having a secure job, and is **unwilling** to delay rewards too long.

Dependence on Others. A high potential manager is **not** greatly concerned with gaining approval from superiors or peers and is **unwilling** to change life goals in accordance with reality opportunities.

THE VALUE OF ASSESSMENT TECHNIQUES

On what basis did the assessment staff make judgments of the foregoing characteristics? Which of the assessment techniques were most helpful? Unfortunately, the analyses needed for definitive answers to these questions are not yet completed and will not be for some time. This is because many narrative reports of behavior in the assessment exercises remain to be coded quantitatively.

The results available have been reported in the professional literature (Bray and Grant, 1966). Before summarizing them, however, it is necessary to point out a serious shortcoming. Some of the assessment techniques have been studied much more fully than others. At the extremes, the In-Basket has been given only one rating (overall quality), whereas the Interview has been rated on eighteen variables. A final comparison of the value of the two techniques will obviously have to wait until a more thorough study of the In-Basket has been completed.

With these qualifications, let us summarize the assessment techniques most important in making judgments of the seven clusters of managerial characteristics. (Statistical data are presented in Table A of the Appendix.)

Judgments of **administrative skills** are determined most strongly by performance on the In-Basket.

Evaluations of **interpersonal skills** depend most heavily on behavior as seen in the group exercises.

Ratings of **intellectual ability** are, of course, quite directly influenced by scores on paper-and-pencil ability tests.

Judgments of **stability of performance** are most dependent, somewhat surprisingly, on performance in the simulations.

Work motivation is seen most clearly in the projective tests and the interview, with additional contributions from the simulations.

Career orientation is strongly apparent in the projective tests and interview reports; it is in connection with this factor that personality questionnaires make their only important contribution to assessment judgments.

Judgments of **dependency on others** rest most heavily on the projective test reports.

These results lead to the conclusion that all the assessment techniques except the personality questionnaires made a substantial contribution to assessment staff judgments. Although two scores on one questionnaire did correlate well with judgments of career orientation, they did not really add anything to the information provided by the projective test reports and the interview. Once again, however, a word of caution is in order. The analysis used merely the separate scores on the questionnaires. If the questionnaires were handled differently, perhaps more value would emerge. For example, judges could rate the management variables from an inspection of all the scores on the questionnaires and without any other information. These ratings could then be compared with the overall assessment judgments. This step is planned as part of the future complete analysis of the assessment center process.

CONCLUDING REMARKS

This chapter has been concerned with the two most important determinants of progress in management—the characteristics of the individual, and the nature of the total opportunity situation surrounding the individual. We have seen that both are indeed significant.

As far as practical implications are concerned, there is a simple prescription for organizations which want college recruits to move up readily in management: hire graduates with good potential and make sure that their assignments and their bosses provide substantial job challenge. Such advice hardly represents a revolutionary new theory; it is, in fact, time worn. Even so, few organizations carry out the plan, although many shout it from the house tops.

The prescription is simple and its implementation is known. Implementation, however, is a matter requiring considerably more resources than are usually devoted to the selection and career development of young managers. Added staff is required for the use of assessment techniques, the selection and training of first bosses, and the monitoring of assignments for challenge. Yet since the failure of management recruits is a hidden cost, the needed staff is seldom made available.

8

Joseph F. Rychlak

LIFE THEMES: ENLARGERS
AND ENFOLDERS

Progress, or lack of it, may well have been a central concern of many of the recruits, but the job was not their whole life. The annual interviews conducted with the men during the eight-year period between assessment and reassessment covered other aspects of their experience, such as family, community activities, and leisure pursuits. This series of interview reports provided for each man a running account of the significant events in his life and the matters that were of concern to him.

The analysis of the many interviews proved to be a formidable task. A selection had to be made of the dimensions along which the material was to be coded. This decision was preceded by a reading of a sizable fraction of the reports to let the materials, in a way, speak for themselves. A second step was to define each dimension and to provide examples so that the interview content could be reliably scored. This preparation of a scoring manual was based on the reading of 352 interviews. Finally, more than 1200 interview reports (running approximately ten pages each) had to be read and scored for all dimensions (Rychlak and Bray, 1967).

The dimensions decided on were nine "life themes" that were represented in nearly all the separate interviews. Each theme was rated on a seven-point scale according to how important the theme appeared to be in the subject's life at the time of the interview. On the scale, a rating of 7 was the highest possible score, 1 the lowest, and 4 was average.

The first theme was *Occupational*. It covers all statements made by the subject concerning his work life, including not only comments about job content but about supervisors, raises or the likelihood thereof, promotions, and attitude toward the company. Figure 1 represents the involvement of one subject on this theme. His initial interview (at the time of first assessment) clearly revealed a less-than-average involvement with the occupational area of life. Concern with the job rose very rapidly during the next three years, however, reaching a high level and remaining there. A review of the man's interviews outlines the content behind these ratings.

This man was a management trainee at the time of first assessment. Because of this he was forced to sit behind a desk, which he found very distasteful. He was already talking about leaving the company. By the following year he had been moved out into the field as an engineer, was in the office only a very few hours a week, and was beginning to see a possible future in the telephone company. One additional year later he was happily putting in an average of 60 hours a week.

As time went on the subject worked even longer hours, so much so that there was a question as to whether it might not be affecting his health, but this did not really influence his job involvement. As a matter of fact, the minor fluctuations in his high rating on the occupational theme were due to some question in his mind that he might find a more challenging job with another company. Nevertheless, by the time of the interview seven years after assessment the young man was reasonably satisfied. In spite of the fact that he had not yet reached middle management, and there was no assurance that he would, he stated that he was "happy about the way my career has gone. I would like to advance faster, but I have been treated fairly."

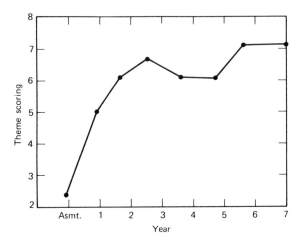

Figure 1   Occupational Life Theme, One Subject.

The second life theme was *Ego Functional*. It refers to concerns about the condition and development of the personal ego—one's mind and body. Included are self-development activities such as broadened reading, educational pursuits, and exercise to improve or maintain physical condition. Such concerns do not necessarily imply egocentricity or conceit. Concern with disease or disability results in higher scores. Figure 2 illustrates the involvement of one of the recruits on this theme. At the time of initial assessment this subject showed somewhat above-average Ego Functional involvement. This involvement declined rather steadily over the next seven years, however, and involvement was quite low by the time of the final interview prior to reassessment. Some summary comments about the content of his interviews follow.

At the outset of the Study this man seemed more intro-spective and intellectually motivated than the average subject. He spoke of having broad interests in the problems of life and had a lifelong history of doing well in school. During his second interview he reported that he had joined a Great Books Club and spoke of wanting to continue educating himself. The fourth interview and the fifth showed a definite decline in such intentions. He had read very few new books and had, in fact, discontinued his Great Books Club discussion. He stated that he had never really enjoyed it. It appeared that the subject was no longer interested in any self-development, but was focusing on the job sphere. He stated that he had not read any books during the previous year and that the amount of time he spent watching television had risen.

The third theme was *Financial-Acquisitive*. It refers to the accumulation of wealth or material possessions such as real estate (including desire to have an impressive home), stocks and bonds, and expensive automobiles. Concern with having enough money to make ends meet also results in higher scores. Figure 3 reveals the

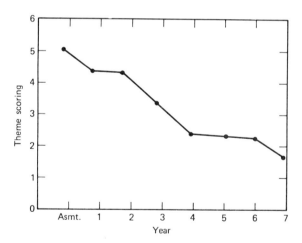

Figure 2. Ego Functional Life Theme, One Subject.

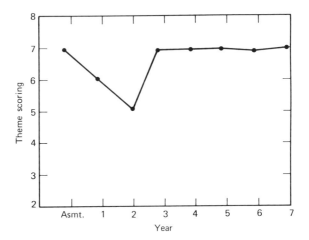

Figure 3   Financial–Acquisitive Life Theme, One Subject.

high involvement of one recruit on this theme. Some of the reasons for his high scores are indicated in the following brief summary:

> In his very first interview this man stated that he wanted money and a lot of it. When asked what he planned to do with it, he flatly said that he would like to have fifteen or twenty suits at a time, have a summer home, a least one new car every year, etc. Four years later he told the interviewer that he wanted more money and an important job, too. He mentioned that he had charge accounts at the best eating spots, and the interviewer was convinced that he was living at a high level and doing it quite successfully. Although he denied any desire to be rich, he left no doubt that his home, standard of living, and style of recreation had to be well above average.

The fourth theme was *Locale-Residential*. It includes comments on the type of location in which one lives and the kind of housing. Figure 4 shows the involvement of one subject on this theme. The obviously dramatic aspect of the trend line is the great leap

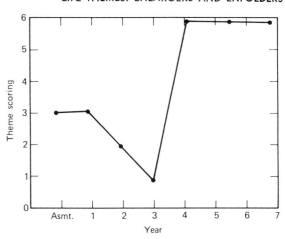

Figure 4   Locale–Residential Life Theme, One Subject.

to a high level of involvement during the fifth interview. The following summary indicates the reason for the change:

This man was living at home at the time the Study started. Immediately after marriage he moved into an apartment with his bride. He was not happy about living in the city, but they continued to be apartment dwellers for several years. The big change in the subject's involvement appeared with the purchase of a home in the suburbs. The house was not new and the recruit started putting in a great deal of work getting it just the way he liked it. This included painting, lawn work, plumbing and electrical changes, etc. The subject was elected an officer of a homeowners' association. He and his wife turned down some opportunities to participate in community groups because they wanted to spend the lion's share of their time on the house.

The fifth theme was *Marital-Familial*. It encompasses preoccupations and activities concerned with the subject's spouse, including in-law matters. It also covers premarital relationships such as dating and engagement. One recruit made no bones about the fact that his family came first, as Figure 5 shows.

This man pointed out in his first interview that he would certainly put family considerations above the job. He stated that when the job begins to affect your family relations, or your health, you are being overly conscientious. This man was the father of a large family by the time of reassessment and reported that he spent much time every evening helping his wife and playing with the children. He reports that his marriage has been a happy one, everything that he could have expected.

The sixth theme was *Parental-Familial*. It subsumes references to parents, siblings, relatives on the parents' side, and involvement in activities deriving from the parents' home. Figure 6 presents the involvement of a subject on this theme. He was above average in his involvement at the time of his assessment interview and later became much more so.

This man was an only child and did not marry during the years covered by these interviews. During the early years

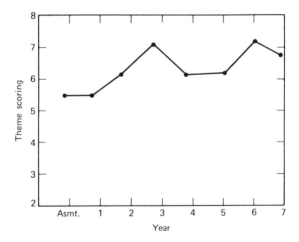

Figure 5   Marital–Familial Life Theme, One Subject

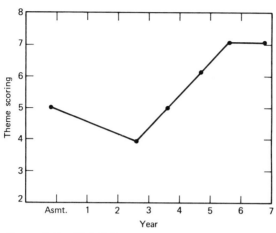

Figure 6   Parental–Familial Life Theme, One Subject.

of the Study he was in the Army. When he returned, he decided to build a home for himself even though he was not married. No sooner did he get it completed than he was transferred. As luck would have it his new assignment brought him within a hundred miles of his home so that it was possible to go home on weekends. This he chose to do, renewing acquaintances with such old friends as had not married, engaging in hobby activities with his parents, helping his father with household construction activities, etc.

The seventh theme was *Recreational-Social*. It focuses on leisure time pursuits, including hobbies, sports, partying, and socializing. Figure 7 shows the course of involvement on this theme for one recruit. He was originally involved only to an average degree and dropped off to a lower level as the years went on.

At the time of the first interview this man mentioned that he had just taken up golf, that he bowled regularly, went to ball games, played the violin, and had reactivated his coin collection. During the following years these activities trailed off into very little time spent on any of them. This decline

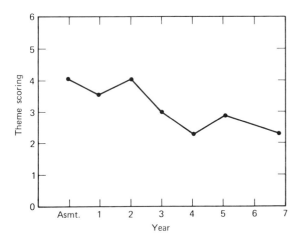

Figure 7   Recreational–Social Life Theme, One Subject.

seemed to be related to his involvement with his wife's family. This was a large gregarious group which lived nearby. They spent a great deal of time with each other, dropping in to watch television and have a few beers together. (Such socializing would not be scored on the Recreational-Social theme since it was done with relatives and would thus be scored on Marital-Familial.)

The eighth theme was *Religious-Humanism*. It has to do with ethical and humanistic involvements which do not need to be part of an organized religion—they need only represent concern with a philosophy of life that acts as an ethic. Figure 8 indicates the involvement on this theme of a man who started out the Study at a high level and, with one brief change of course, declined to a very low level. The following summary of interview comments shows the nature of this change.

This man impressed the initial assessment interviewer as a man with strong humanistic needs which were being expressed outside of organized religion. Prior to joining the

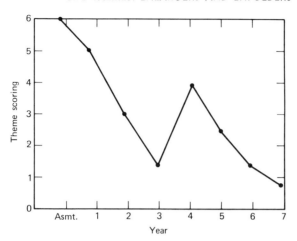

Figure 8   Religious–Humanism Life Theme, One Subject.

business, he had had some disturbing experiences in the Korean War which impelled him into the study of man's legal and moral structures. He reported spending six to eight months in reading law books and actually started the formal study of law. He found this was not what he wanted, however, and took philosophy courses instead. Unfortunately, he did not find what he was seeking and seemed to decide that no answers were possible. At the end of the interviewing years prior to reassessment, he had arrived at a competitive, somewhat "dog-eat-dog" point of view.

The ninth, and final, theme was *Service*. It has to do with community activities such as the Chamber of Commerce, Boy Scouts, and political parties. It excludes church activities, which are scored under Religious-Humanism. Figure 9 plots the varying course of involvement on the Service theme of one of the recruits, whose originally average involvement progressed to a very high point during the eight years of interviewing but returned to average at the end of the period. These changes were influenced by his job and family.

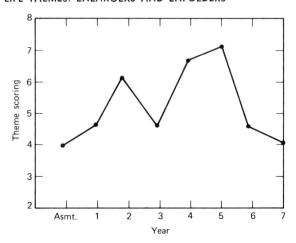

Figure 9   Service Life Theme, One Subject.

This man originally mentioned that he would like to join the Junior Chamber of Commerce some day; he did not appear to be any more than average in his interest in service. Soon thereafter he married a girl who was very interested in self-development and expressive activities. By the third year he was in the Chamber of Commerce and took major roles in both the Red Cross organization and the Community Chest drive. The following year saw him somewhat less involved due to the birth of his first child. This drop was short-lived, however. He soon was involved in the Rotary, Toastmasters', the Chamber of Commerce, the United Fund, Junior Achievement, and on committees for the local symphony and hospital improvement. His wife also continued outside the home activities. At this point the subject was transferred to another community where there was far less to do. His involvement in service activities declined, but at the end of the period his attention seemed to be turning to participation in church matters.

GROUP TRENDS

Some men, as the preceding examples illustrate, fluctuated widely in their involvement on the various life themes. As has been seen, however, some of these fluctuations were the result of almost accidental influences, such as a change of work location. To determine the usual, or average, course of life involvements for the recruits, it is necessary to examine the group trends. Figure 10 presents these average trends for all nine themes.

All life themes but one show some significant trend. Three of the themes indicate a definite upward trend—Occupational, Financial-Acquisitive, and Marital-Familial. Such developments are, of course, quite reasonable. Employment with the Bell System was the start of a lifelong career for most of the recruits. It would be surprising if involvement with the occupational area of life did not grow during the early years on the job. As a matter of fact, the increase in involvement is quite small. A much steeper rise might have been expected. The steady rise in Marital-Familial and Financial-Acquisitive involvement is the expected result of marriages, growing families, and the need to attend to these added responsibilties.

Four themes show a significant downward trend: Parental-Familial, Ego Functional, Service, and Recreational-Social. The first of these decreasing involvements is, once again, highly understandable. In some instances job location or deciding to live in one's wife's community put considerable distance between the recruit and his parents. Even when distance was a less important factor, the recruit's own family and his in-laws often reduced interaction with parents. And, of course, some parents died during this period.

The decline in Ego Functional, Service, and Recreational-Social themes were more surprising. One might have pictured the young management trainee as digging into self-development, getting involved in the community as an enhancement of his managerial image, and expanding his social life through new friends made on the job. This energetic picture is not borne out by the interviews. Recreational-Social involvement declined steadily throughout the

94

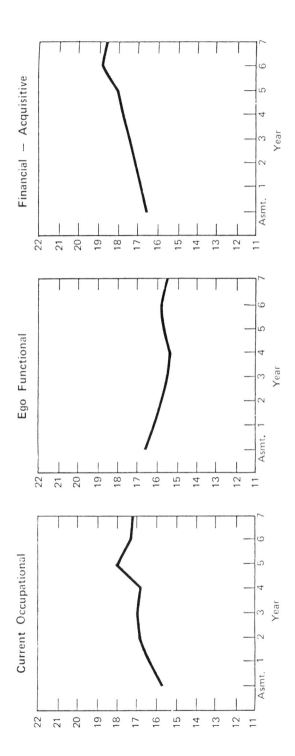

Figure 10 Life Themes—Total Group Trends.

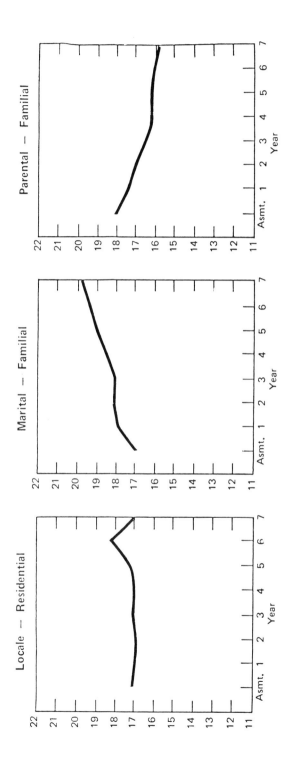

Figure 10 (continued)

96

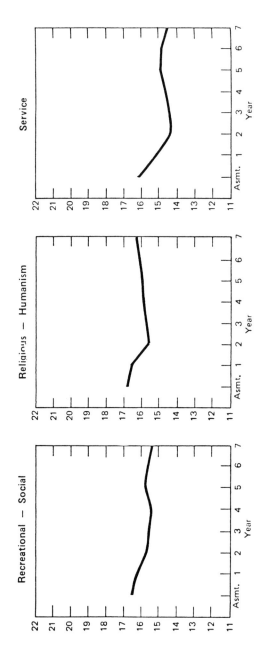

Recreational — Social

Religious — Humanism

Service

Year

See Table B (Appendix) For Data

Figure 10 (continued)

period. (It must be remembered, however, that activities solely with relatives were not scored on this theme.) Ego Functional and Service involvements declined sharply during the first three to four years of the Study, although the declines do not appear to continue.

The Religious-Humanism factor exhibited a significant decline during the early years, but like Ego Functional and Service, there was no further decline, and even a slight tendency to rise. The Locale-Residential theme, perhaps somewhat surprisingly, showed no general response to marriages, growing families, or job transfers.

LIFE THEMES AND SUCCESS

The results just presented were those for the total group of recruits. As we saw in earlier chapters, some of the recruits had already reached the minimum goal projected for them at the time of employment—the third level of management—whereas others had not and perhaps never would. It seems logical that success on the job or the lack of it would be related to life style. Perhaps, for example, the successful man puts most of himself into his work and does little in the way of community service. Or the unsuccessful man may turn to recreational and social life with a vengeance.

In order to examine such possibilities, life theme trends were computed for two contrasting groups. One consisted of all the men who had reached third level management or higher by the time of reassessment. The other was an equal sized group made up of all those who had not advanced above the first level of management and a random sample of those at second level. Figure 11 presents the trend of involvements on each of the life themes for the two groups.

A most dramatic difference is seen in the Occupational theme. The more successful men had more involvement on this theme right at the outset of the Study and continued to become more involved as the years passed. The less successful men started at a lower level, declined, and at the end of this interviewing period were at a decidedly low level. This decline was interrupted during

98

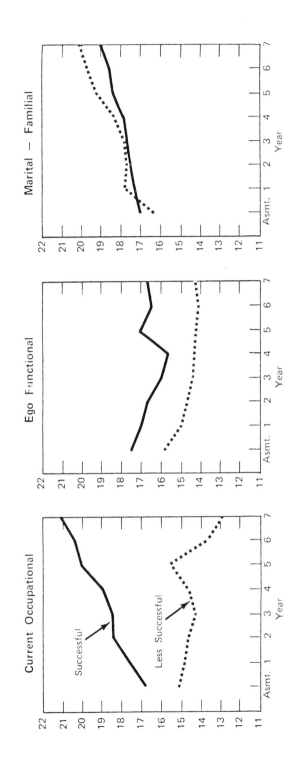

Figure 11 Life Themes—Comparisons of Those Who Did and Did Not Reach Middle Management.

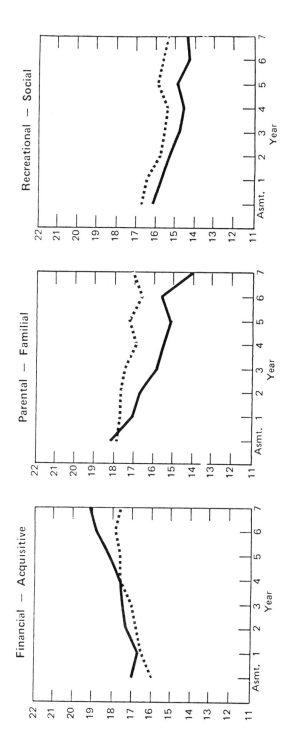

Figure 11 (continued)

99

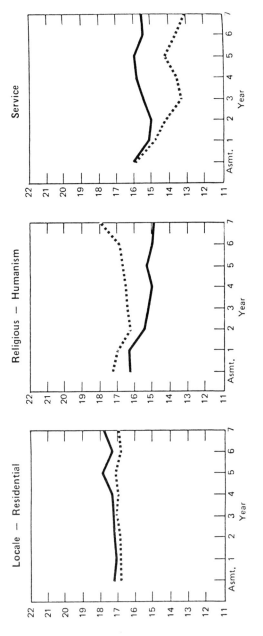

100

See Table C (Appendix) For Data

Figure 11 (continued)

the fourth and fifth interviewing years by a definite advance. The reasons for this temporary rise are not clear.

The Ego Functional (self-development) theme also showed a difference between the two groups right from the outset, with the more successful group showing more involvement. This relatively greater activity was continued over the course of the years, although the successful men showed the same decline as the less successful during the earlier part of the period. There is a suggestion that the successful group is increasing in involvement during the last three years.

A third theme to show a decided difference in favor of the successful group is Service. Here there was no difference between the two groups at the beginning; but a quite large discrepancy developed within three years, and it persisted through the years prior to reassessment.

The less successful individuals showed more involvement and a different trend on two themes. One of these was Parental-Familial. Here the two groups started off at almost exactly the same level, but the more successful men declined quickly and sharply, whereas the less successful men declined very gradually. There was a substantial difference between the groups at the time of the last interview in this series.

The other theme showing more involvement on the part of the less successful group was Religious-Humanism—the less successful were somewhat more involved at the outset, but the two groups exhibited almost exactly the same declining trend during the next two years of interviews. Then, however, the less successful men started a gradual but accelerating rise on this theme, while the more successful continued a slow decline.

One additional theme that deserves mention is Marital-Familial, since the less successful group shows a steeper rise in involvement than the more successful men. This difference in trend did not quite reach statistical significance, but it is consistent with the greater activity of the less successful men on the Parental-Familial theme.

The remaining themes—Financial-Acquisitive, Locale-Residential, and Recreational-Social—revealed no statistically significant differences between the two groups either in overall level of activity or trend.

The differences between the life styles of the successful and less successful recruits become somewhat clearer if a further refinement in the groups is made. In this refinement the "true positive" group includes those who impressed *both* the assessment staff and the telephone company management as having high potential; more specifically, this group is composed of those predicted by the assessment staff to reach middle management who did reach this level by the time of reassessment. The other group for this analysis, the true negative, comprises those whom the assesssment staff predicted would not reach middle management and who in fact had not reached this level by the time of reassessment. Figure 12 presents the life theme trends for these two contrasting groups.

All the themes except Locale-Residential show interesting differences. Very striking is the comparison of the two groups on the Occupational theme. The true positive group was considerably more involved in work even at the time of first assessment, rising steadily and substantially throughout the period. The consistently less successful men were much less involved at the outset and, except the hard-to-explain surge at the sixth year, generally declined, finishing with even less involvement than they had initially displayed.

The true positive group was significantly higher at the very beginning on the the Ego Functional and Financial-Acquisitive themes. Although both groups declined on Ego Functional rather similarly during the earliest years, the more successful group showed an upward trend later. The less successful men wound up quite lower than their starting point. Both groups showed a parallel upward movement on the Financial-Acquisitive theme, with the gap between them remaining just about the same throughout the interviewing period.

The Service theme, while ultimately revealing a positive relationship with success, contrasts with the above-mentioned themes by showing no early difference between the two groups. It is not until the fourth interviewing year that the groups break apart clearly, with the successful men showing a mild gain and the less successful a sharp drop. The successful men finished the interviewing years almost where they had started; the less successful were considerably lower.

The four remaining themes—Marital-Familial, Parental-Familial, Recreational-Social, and Religious-Humanism—are similar in that they indicate no original difference between the groups but considerable difference at the end of the period, with the less successful men being more highly involved. These differences are particularly marked in the case of the Parental-Familial and Religious-Humanism themes.

ENLARGING VERSUS ENFOLDING LIFE STYLES

The results just summarized suggest two contrasting life styles— that of the "Enlarger" and that of the "Enfolder." The enlarging life style is oriented toward the goals of innovation, change, and growth. The Enlarger moves away from tradition and places his emphasis on adaptation, self-development, and the extension of influence outward, into the work and community spheres. The Enlarger looks for responsibility on the job and is likely also to seek and achieve a position of influence in service organizations. Self-development activities are stressed; thus Enlargers are likely not only to read, attend the theatre, and keep up with current events, but they take night courses and even respond to the promptings of physical fitness and health food buffs. At the same time, their earlier ties to parents and formal religious practices begin to weaken. The Enlarger finds that his values have changed so dramatically that he no longer enjoys the company of old friends in the neighborhoods of his childhood. Except for a certain nostalgia when he visits parents and relatives, he is not satisfied with the ties of yesterday. A complete commitment to one religion is similarly less meaningful, particularly since he makes every effort to see alternative points of view and to lend himself to new experiences of all varieties. This does not mean that he breaks off from his church entirely, of course, but that also happens.

The enfolding life style is oriented to the goals of tradition, stability, and inward strength. Rather than pitching his influence outward, the Enfolder seeks to cultivate and solidify that which

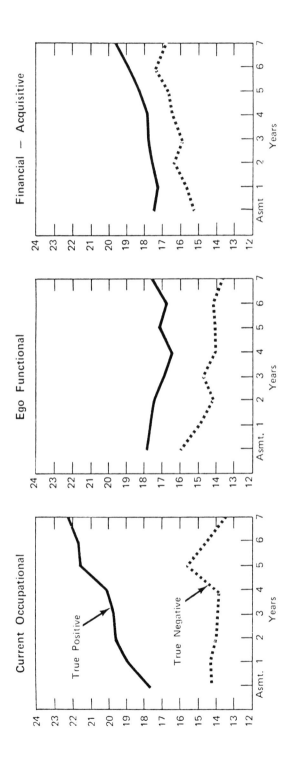

Figure 12 Life Theme Trends—Comparisons of True Positives and True Negatives.

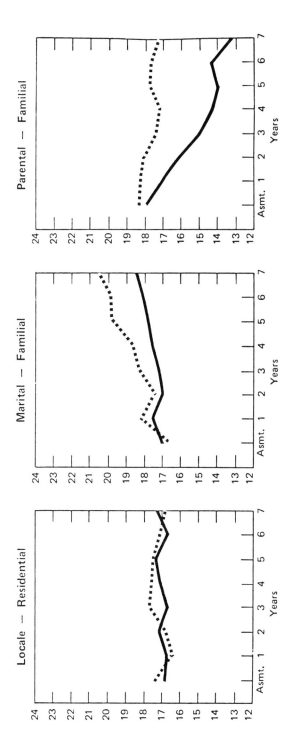

Figure 12 (continued)

105

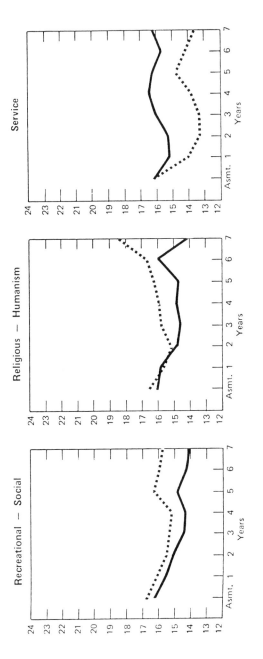

See Table D (Appendix) For Data

Figure 12 (continued)

106

invites attention within his more familiar sphere. He is not a "joiner" of social or community organizations, and when he does enter into such activities he rarely seeks an active role. On the other hand, he may be quite active in his church, or in Boy Scout troops or Little League teams that have their origins in the church community. His "good works" are usually tied to his church affiliation. He values parental ties and seeks to keep a relationship active with boyhood chums, if this is at all possible. He may find it quite upsetting to leave the home town area, even if the move portends job advancement. In a new locale he is likely to have considerable difficulty feeling "at home." He is not likely to attend night college or to study on his own time unless he feels assured that his effort will bring direct job rewards. He may begin a self-improvement program, but his heart is seldom in it, or he begins it later than the next man and usually stops it sooner. He likes to settle into a job and see it through to a full conclusion, getting great satisfaction from a job well done. He is not awed by fads and usually senses that not enough people today "count their blessings." He forms close attachments to a small circle of friends, and most of his socializing is done with relatives. Status considerations sometimes embarrass him, and he values informality, sincerity, and genuineness in human affairs.

The enlarging and enfolding life styles are only hypothetical types, but they serve to sum up many of the observations encompassed in the numerous interviews on which this chapter is based. As the life theme trend data show, the enlarging life style is more prevalent among the recruits who were definitely successful on the job. Job success does not, of course, guarantee happiness. There were just as many unhappy Enlargers as Enfolders—if not more!

A CORPORATE CASE HISTORY: THE ENFOLDER

A better appreciation of the enfolding and enlarging life styles can be gained by more detailed case histories. Thus, two composite portraits have been put together, each built around at least a dozen of the recruits. The following is the picture of an Enfolder.

The subject was a 26-year-old college graduate when he accepted employment in the telephone company, beginning in the Plant Department. He chose to come with Bell primarily on the advice of his brother, who is a long-time employee of the company. He also wanted to be with a large firm which could provide him with training and development opportunities in a variety of management positions. Finally, he saw the people who worked for the company as friendly and considerate, and he liked them.

He is the third son in a family of five children, with a younger sister being the "baby" of the family. He describes his childhood in pleasant, albeit uneventful, terms. He has great respect for his father, and his oldest brother (who recommended the telephone company) is kind of a hero to him. He was not too close to his mother during his childhood, although he loves her very much and still sees a great deal of her. His most pleasant memories stem from the hunting and fishing trips he took with his dad and his brothers. They still do a lot together, and he can always count on his brothers for anything he might need to have done—car repairs, buying things at a discount, and so forth. They always give him a hand, and they know that he is always available for requests on his time or financial resources when they need him.

Following high school this man and three school buddies enlisted together in the Air Force. He spent some time in Europe during a three-year hitch but did not find it particularly enjoyable. He had not really planned to attend college, but jobs were scarce when he returned home from the service, and he could see the writing on the wall—a man was not going to go far without a college degree. He was engaged to his high school sweetheart by this time, and with the help of his fiancée's family as well as his own parents and some GI benefits, he completed college as a business administration major. He married during his sophomore year, and their first child was born in his senior year. His grades were slightly above average in college, and he felt that he had benefited from this additional schooling. The wife did not attend, preferring to work while she could to help them along financially.

At the assessment center this man impressed the staff as fairly relaxed and not introspective. He was quite problem oriented in our group problems, as in the manufacturing task, where he briefly was looked to for leadership because of the sheer effort he directed at getting the job done. However, his impulsiveness and lack of ability to coordinate the overall picture cost him the leadership in short order. In the discussion group he seemed unable to make his thinking clear to his peers, although at times he made excellent points and had considerable reserves of practical, common sense. His In-Basket performance was rather poor, showing weaknesses in planning and organization as well as decisiveness. Ability tests suggest a fairly intelligent person, with remarkably little grasp of current events.

This man's work career has centered on the Plant Department, with some time also spent in Accounting. He has proven to be a good technician and a reliable worker, but there is little to say for his management skills; at reassessment, in fact, he still carried the first level management rank with which he had begun the Study some eight years earlier. At initial assessment he had predicted a District (third) level job by ten years, and at least a Division (fourth) level rank by retirement. At the time of reassessment he was somewhat defensive about his lack of promotion but retained a fairly good humor about it—blaming it on "the breaks" and a couple of foolish reservations he had voiced early in his career.

It seems that he had been reluctant to take transfers in the past, especially during times of family stress—when his wife was near delivery in a pregnancy (they now have four children), when his father was about to have an operation, and so forth. The couple have had to move four times in the past eight years, and even though they were distantly removed from their parents on only one of these occasions, neither he nor his wife have been happy with the company's seeming policy of uprooting its managers every few years. Peers and superiors have told him in the past that his attitude is not conducive to upward mobility on the job, but he had not been able to see their point at the time. It seemed to him that it was in the company's interest to keep their employees happy.

He found his early job training a rather dull affair and was elated when finally given his first real work assignment. He hates to read, preferring to learn by doing, and nothing gives him more satisfaction than seeing a job through to a successful conclusion. This man's life style has always stressed security—the steady accumulation of desirables such as a car, furniture, and then a house. He values a rich family life, loves to play with his children, and seems to be a perfect husband and father. Most of his socializing centers around either the wife's or his parental family members. He has never taken a night college course of any sort, and his reading is confined to newspapers—especially the sports pages. He spends a good deal of time before the television set. He likes to grow things and apparently has quite a green thumb (the family put in a full garden each summer). He also has a woodworking shop and has built some of his home furnishings from scratch. The wife seems to be a loving mother. She defers to her husband on most decisions, although he lets her manage the family finances. He once told us that he did not really know what his precise yearly salary was—his wife took the check each week and "that was it." He comes into the major decisions of the family, and it is a point of honor that he "wears the pants" in the home.

This man has never been active in community organizations such as the Junior Chamber of Commerce or related, nondenominational civic groups. He has, however, been quite active in his church. He is an usher and has always participated in charity organizations as well as financial drives. He plans on becoming active in a Boy Scout troop that meets in the church hall when his eldest son becomes interested in such activities.

At reassessment this man was little changed with respect to general management ability. If anything, he appeared more aloof and less decisive than he had been initially. He is still in need of, and hopeful about attaining, promotion to a higher level, but he did not wish to state specific goals. He has thought about leaving the Bell System to enter his own business, but he lacks capital and has some doubts about whether the move would be worth the risk. Since his salary advances have been quite good, he now finds that he has been "priced out of the market" with respect to most of the other companies that might have hired him. In many ways he believes himself to be a success in life, in view of his happy home life, good health, and satisfying work (for he does like the actual work that he does). One could not consider this man to be unhappy, except in the sense that he feels somewhat embarrassed about his lack of advancement. We suspect that were he to reach second level he would feel greatly relieved and would continue at a decent work pace until retirement. We also suspect that this is the most he hopes for on the work front.

A COMPOSITE CASE HISTORY: THE ENLARGER

The subject was 27 years of age when he began with the Bell System, having just earned a degree in Engineering. Following his interdepartmental training, this man worked as a Central Office Foreman for one year and was quickly promoted to second level as an Assistant PBX Supervisor. Within another year he was picked to fill a vacancy at District level as an Outside Plant and Station Supervisor. The latter position was a staff assignment, in which he was called on to funnel various data and reports up the hierarchy to higher level personnel. Apparently he gained considerable visibility in the process and did an outstanding job as well. After roughly two years of this assignment he was rotated back into the field, as a District Plant Manager. He first managed a small district and then was given a larger one, since he seemed quite capable of meeting every challenge. By about the seventh year of his employment this man was promoted to Division (fourth) level, as an Area Plant Supervisor. This is a staff position, in which he has charge of statewide budgets and policies.

Although this man's commitment to the job sphere has been great, he has from the very first considered job advancement as only one aspect of his personal development. He is easily one of the most career-oriented men of our sample, and a job setting is merely one aspect of the broader picture. His planfulness was apparent as far back as college, where he concluded that he was not in the true sense of the word interested in engineering. He did not like the work *per se,* but he knew that the training would be an excellent background for management. He was a good but not outstanding student. He was also atypical of engineering students in that he placed great emphasis on liberal arts electives, purchased a set of the Great Books upon graduation to continue his self-broadening efforts, and constantly presses himself to exceed the routine activities of daily life. For years he did not purchase a television set "on principle."

At the initial assessment he made an impressive record. He became the unquestioned leader in both the group problems, showing insightful grasps of the jobs to be done. He reflected excellent organizing ability, as well as readiness for decisiveness and even a certain authoritarian aggressiveness when the situation called for it. In the main, however, he was considerate and tactful. He had projected the District level in seven years at original assessment but had made no career predictions. The assessment staff felt that this man was less motivated by financial considerations than by the desire to prove himself capable. His intellectual abilities were above average, although he was not the brightest of the recruits. He was, however, among the most well-informed men with regard to current events.

Before enrolling in college, this man had served three years (all in the United States) as a company clerk and supply sergeant in the Army. His family background includes an older brother and a younger sister. He feels that he had always been closer to his mother than his father while a child. The mother always was ready with moral support, and she took him into her confidence as if he were her equal on many points. It is only in more recent years that he has felt more relaxed with his father. He was always on good terms with his brother, but since the latter was a few years older than he, they had little in common. He has great regard for his sister and is pleased that she has recently completed college near the top of her class. He was mildly critical of his brother for having flunked out of college.

Although this man had planned to extend his education through night school, job demands have kept him from completing the master's degree in business administration that he set out to obtain. He was able to earn about 12 credit hours over the years, however, and he has kept up a rather steady reading schedule, including both management and current fiction offerings. His wife, whom he met at college, was an English major, and since she loves to read, he is kept well informed on the latest developments in literature. He also reads widely in the newspaper and subscribes to a few news magazines. The couple have two children and have recently purchased their first home. He had to move his family five times over the run of our Study, hence the relatively late investment in a house.

The marital adjustment of this young man has not always been perfect. One factor was the unhappiness of the wife's parents with the many and distant moves the couple had to make. And although the wife was intellectually prepared to help her husband advance, she seems to be somewhat dependent, and at one time she found the time commitments he was making rather threatening. He would dash in from the job and then dash out to his night course, and so forth. She became depressed and stayed with her parents for a few months after their first child was born. Long evenings of discussion eventually worked things out, along about the fifth follow-up year. There was never any question about his devotion to her, or vice versa. Making Division level was also so rewarding—even to his in-laws—that the sacrifices and dedication all seem worth it now to everyone concerned. At the same time, this man continues to ask himself precisely what he wants out of life and whether "this is it." He is thus unwilling to consider himself unalterably committed to the Bell System, even at this point in time. He said, "I don't want to be locked in," but he so enjoys what he is doing that he cannot think of an alternative worth pursuing.

He has had other job offers, of course. Although his community involvements are rather modest (PTA, Rotary, etc.), for a while he became quite active in the Junior Chamber of Commerce and was elected chapter president. Through contacts made in the service organization he was offered other jobs but never gave them serious consideration because they seemed no better than his present position, and he was always doing well enough on the job.

He has gradually drifted away from contacts with his parents. His wife keeps up a correspondence with both sets of families, now that they lived some distance away, and he is naturally interested in knowing what is taking place. He no longer considers himself to be a member of the older circles, however; he fully accepts that one "cannot go home again." When he meets former pals, and even when he is visiting his parents, he feels somehow in a different world. He is nostalgic about the old days, and he loves his people, but after a brief visit to them in their world, he is anxious to return to his own.

He attends church less often now. His wife would like to increase their attendance, and as the children grow older he may return to a more active role in his faith. But at the present time he cannot feel an honest need for the formal aspects of religion. He takes his family to services on certain major holidays, and they attend with their parents when the family gets together. He has no great doubts concerning the validity of a belief in God, but the formal aspects of religion are now without relevance to him.

He likes to socialize occasionally. The couple have many friends in the telephone company, but they also make an effort to cultivate friends who have other professional and occupational identities. They enjoy travel, and each summer he makes a point of going "any place other than visiting my relations" on his vacation. They look forward to much more interesting travel as their children mature.

This man's reassessment was even more excellent and promising than his initial assessment. Since his peers were not unaware of his job status, there is some uncertainty regarding how much of the sophisticated leadership he displayed in the group situations was due to basic ability and how much to his present job title. However, he demonstrated outstanding planning, organization, and decisiveness on the In-Basket as well—which is, of course, a solitary task. His needs for advancement seemed to have increased, overall, and some of the assessment staff members felt that he was a future company president or vice president. Interestingly, in the personal interview, he admitted to periods of depression during which he felt guilty for not having performed as well as he thought he could have.

LIFE STYLES AND SUCCESS

The portraits of the Enlarger and the Enfolder are written at the descriptive level rather than the causal level, but they may imply that a man's style of life is something he carries with him when he joins an organization and that his life themes are but little influenced by job success. Although the Study materials do not allow a final resolution of such "nature or nurture" questions, further light may be thrown on the issue by one final set of comparisons.

Some of the men seen at the original assessment centers were predicted to reach middle management and did reach it. The life themes of these successful men have been presented. Another group of men appeared just as promising at assessment but had not reached middle management by the time of reassessment. Comparing the life theme trends of these two groups may clarify the extent to which life styles are affected by career success. The same type of comparison can be made between those who were predicted not to reach middle management and did not (the less successful group discussed earlier) and those who were predicted not to reach middle management but did, in fact, arrive there before reassessment. The parallel sets of charts are shown in Figure 13.

In discussing these charts, the group whose progress did not match their favorable assessment predictions is called "false positives," and the group who succeeded in spite of negative predictions is called "false negatives." The reader is cautioned not to interpret these terms to mean that the assessment evaluation of the man was necessarily incorrect. As we have seen, progress was dependent on situational as well as personal factors, and some of the false positives, for example, may be quite capable men. It cannot be said, at this point at least, how often the failure of prediction was due to errors at assessment or to the opposite— the failure of the organization to accurately appraise the individual.

For the sake of brevity, comments about these life theme comparisons are presented in summary form.

Occupational. False positives were lower than true positives throughout. In addition, the false positives dropped off sharply after the sixth year. False negatives were not much different from true negatives in the early years, but they increased steadily to finish the period at a much higher level.

116

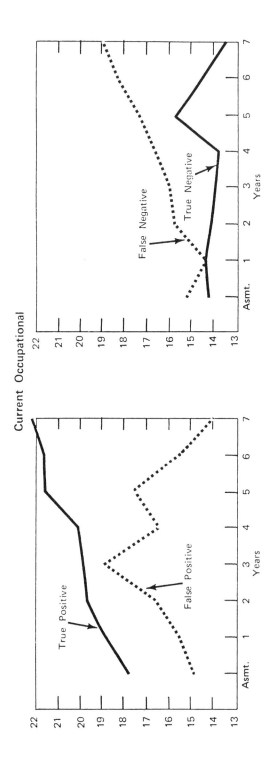

Figure 13 Life Themes—Comparisons of Four Prediction Groups.

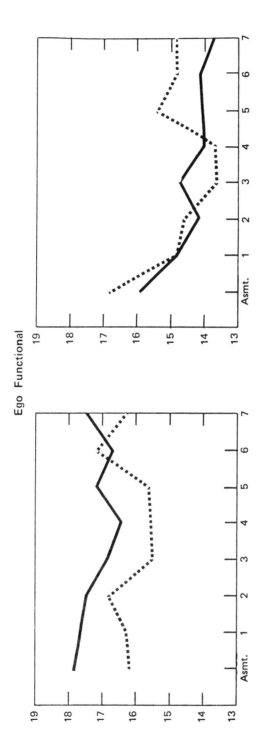

Ego Functional

Figure 13 (continued)

117

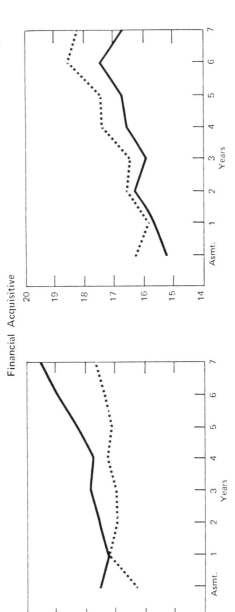

Financial Acquisitive

See Table D (Appendix) For Data

Figure 13 (continued)

Ego Functional. False positives and positives were not very different. False negatives and negatives were also similar, although the false negatives showed a rise in the later years.

Financial-Acquisitive. False positives and positives are not very different until positives accelerated in the last three years. False negatives were somewhat higher than negatives throughout; trend was very similar.

Locale-Residential. False positives were very close to the positives at the start but dropped away from them later. False negatives were higher than the negatives throughout.

Marital-Familial. False positives and positives were highly similar throughout. False negatives and negatives were substantially similar throughout.

Parental-Familial. False positives did not show a sharp drop, as did the positives. False negatives and negatives were similar most of the way, with false negatives exhibiting a sharp late drop.

Recreational-Social. False positives were much higher than the positives throughout. False negatives dropped lower than the negatives late in the period.

Religious-Humanism. False positives were much higher than the positives throughout. False negatives showed an erratic course, but were not consistently different from the negatives.

Service. False positives and positives showed an erratic course but were similar. The false negatives were even more erratic but were similar to the negatives.

The foregoing comparisons suggest several hypotheses. Some of these have to do with the prediction of success, others with the effects of greater or lesser job success on life styles. Regarding prediction, it may be significant that the true positives were much more involved right from the start on the Occupational theme than

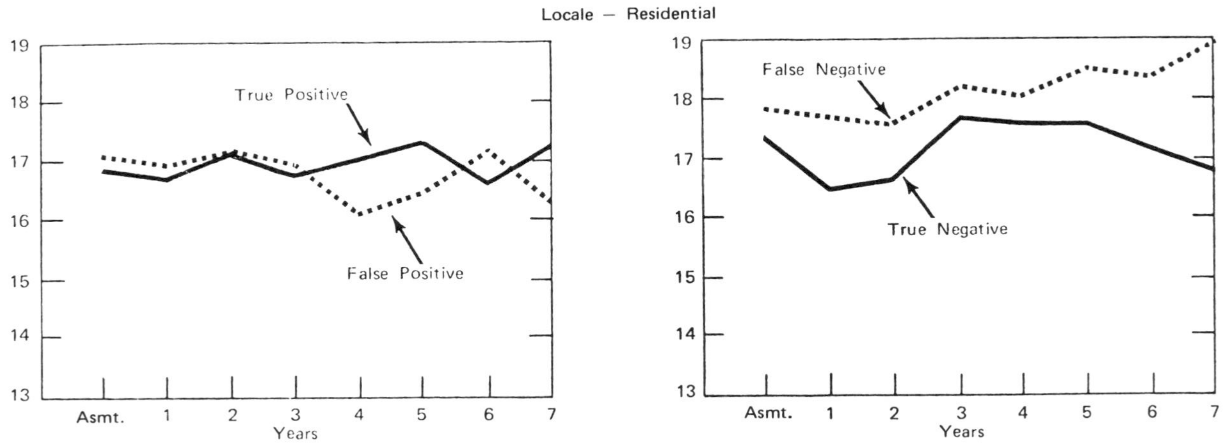

Locale — Residential

Figure 13 (continued)

120

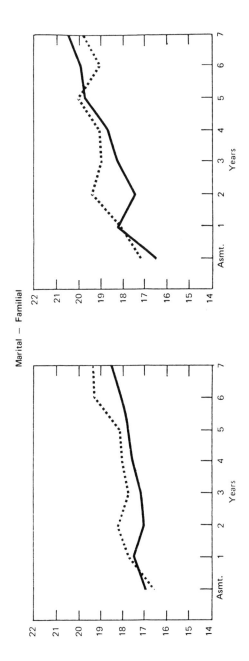

Marital — Familial

Figure 13 (continued)

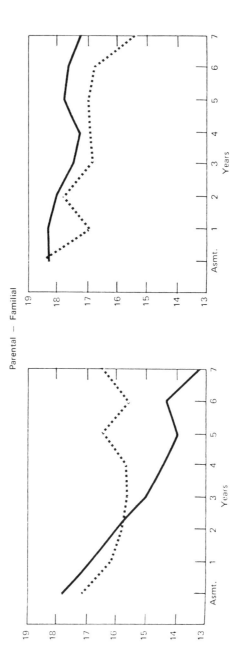

Parental — Familial

See Table D (Appendix) For Data

Figure 13 (continued)

were the false positives. The true positives were also less involved than the false positives on the Recreational-Social and the Religious-Humanism themes. These differences may have implications for prediction. A man who gives a favorable appearance in assessment but who is *not* strongly involved occupationally and *is* highly involved with outside activities may not be a good bet.

Also on the predictive side, the false negatives were more strongly involved on the Financial-Acquisitive and the Locale-Residential themes than the true negatives. Both these themes are served by progress in management, with its resulting greater income. Possibly those who do not shine in assessment but who are "hungry" are more likely to progress than their less materialistic counterparts.

One life theme that is definitely, and not surprisingly, affected by job success is Occupational involvement. Both the true positives and false negatives (i.e., the two groups that got ahead) rose sharply on this theme, whereas both the less successful groups (the true negatives and the false positives) finished lower than they had begun. It seems very clear that success breeds involvement.

The other life theme that seems to be clearly affected by job success is Parental-Familial. The true positives showed a precipitous drop on this theme, and although the false negatives were rather high on the theme for most of the period, they too dropped off decidedly in the final year.

Other effects are not clear for all groups. The true positives, however, did pull away from the false positives on the Financial-Acquisitive and Locale-Residential themes. Once again, success seems to bring greater involvement in the fruits of success. The false negatives eventually rose above the true negatives on Ego Functional and fell below them on Recreational-Social. It may be that success on the job suggests the advisability of becoming more interested in self-development and less interested in fun and games.

Three themes showed no difference in trend between the true positives and the false positives or between the true negatives and the false negatives. These were Marital-Familial, Religious-Humanism, and Service. It appears that these themes are not greatly affected by job success.

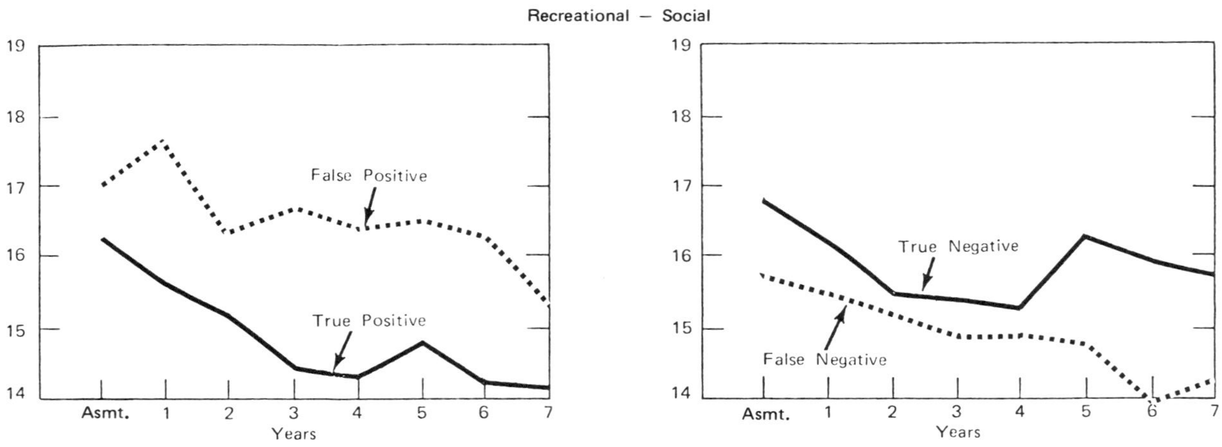

Recreational — Social

Figure 13   (continued)

124

Religious – Humanism

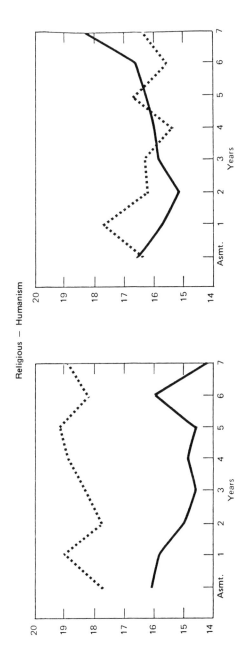

Figure 13 (continued)

125

126

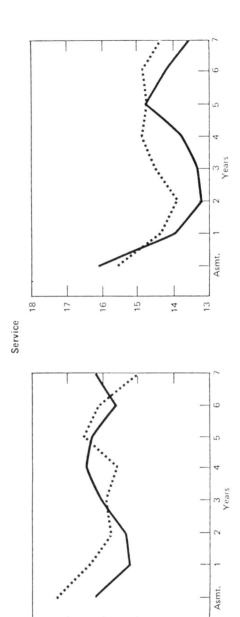

Service

See Table D (Appendix) For Data

Figure 13 (continued)

SUMMARY REMARKS

It is now time to pull together all the various comparisons made previously and to summarize the conclusions that can be drawn from them. These conclusions center around the relationships between life styles and advancement in management.

It appears that a knowledge of the involvement of a management recruit on some of the life themes at the very start of his career would be an aid in predicting how readily he will move along into middle management. These themes are Occupational, Ego Functional, and Financial-Acquisitive. Recruits who are quite concerned about work, want to a higher degree than others the monetary rewards that success at work can bring, and are interested in self-development, are more likely to advance than those less involved in such matters.

Success or lack of it during the early years in business affects involvement on at least seven of the nine life themes. Success has its most pronounced accelerating effect on Occupational involvement. Not only are those who are destined to advance earlier higher on this theme at the very beginning, but their differential involvement is even greater eight years later. Success also has an effect on the Ego Functional theme. It does not forestall an initial decline in self-developmental interests, but it leads to recovery of interest a little later. A similar effect takes place on the theme of Service. The more successful men tend to hold the involvement they have, while the less successful decline.

At the risk of some oversimplification but in the interest of clarity, the main effects of success are summarized as follows:

	More Successful	Less Successful
Occupational	Dramatic gain	Small loss
Ego Functional	Held even	Large loss
Service	Held even	Large loss
Marital-Familial	Moderate gain	Large gain
Parental-Familial	Dramatic loss	Held even
Religious-Humanism	Moderate loss	Moderate gain
Recreational-Social	Sharp loss	Small loss

These results lead to the conclusion that job success holds one to the quite job-related themes of Occupational, Ego Functional, and Service, whereas lack of success permits one, or motivates him, to turn away. Success also militates against outside-work themes, whereas lack of success may permit involvement in them or even drive one to them for life satisfaction.

9

CHANGES IN MANAGEMENT ABILITIES

Management abilities are of two kinds. One has to do with job content. The manager may have more or less knowledge of the technical side of the work he and his subordinates do, about the work of other departments in his company, and about company policies and practices. The other type of management ability consists of management skills; that is, the manager may be more or less capable in face-to-face leadership, planning and organizing, logical reasoning, and communicating effectively.

The assessment centers at the beginning of the Study and those which the recruits attended eight years later were designed to measure management ability of the second type. The intent was to determine how much basic managerial ability each recruit had. There was no attempt to measure, or even to rate, a recruit's knowledge of engineering, central office technology, accounting practices, sales, or any of the many other job contents that make up the operation of a telephone company.

Data presented in earlier chapters show clearly that the measures and ratings of basic management skills obtained at original assessment weighed heavily in the assessment staff's overall evaluation of potential and were predictive of later advancement. Some of the key assessment variables were Scholastic Aptitude, Organizing and Planning, Decision Making, Human Relations Skills, and Behavior Flexibility. Of the seven factors underlying assessment ratings, three were ability factors—intellectual ability, administrative skills, and interpersonal skills.

Organizations characteristically view the early years of management experience as a time of development. Programs for the management recruit often include rotation through a variety of assignments or special opportunities within an assignment to help or force the young hire to grow as a manager. Although part of the intent of such programs is merely to inculcate greater knowledge of the operations of the organization, there is also the strong expectation that basic management ability will be improved. Many line executives believe firmly that managers are made and not born.

Between the time of assessment and reassessment, the recruits in the Management Progress Study had eight years of business experience. They had been called on to think, to administer jobs, and to interact with superiors, peers, and subordinates both formally and informally. Did this experience have any effect on their ability as managers? The answer to this question has important implications for the selection and development of management.

INTELLECTUAL ABILITY

Intelligence is perhaps the one basic management ability that most people would *not* expect to see change during the early years of the career. The once firm teaching of psychometricians that intelligence reaches its maximum in the early teens and then remains essentially constant during the middle years of life still has very wide lay acceptance.

Intellectual ability was measured directly at original assessment by the School and College Ability Test (SCAT), a 110-item multiple-choice test composed of language and quantitative items; and by the Critical Thinking Test, a 50-item multiple-choice test in which the subject is asked to make inferences from verbal, tabular, and graphic material. In addition, each recruit took a 120-item multiple-choice test of knowledge of contemporary affairs. At reassessment the recruits took different forms of the SCAT and the Contemporary Affairs Test and repeated the same form of the Critical Thinking Test. Table 16 shows the average scores on the three tests at the time of assessment and reassessment. In all cases there was a significant increase (1 percent level of confidence) in test score.

The assessment staff rating of intellectual ability, of course, was almost dictated by the scores on the objective tests, particularly the SCAT. It would be expected, therefore, that this rating would show a comparable increase from assessment to reassessment. This was the case, with the upward change again being highly reliable statistically.

Such findings would have been startling even a few years ago, but they no longer surprise measurement specialists. The early studies of the relationships between mental test score and age were based on testing people of various ages rather than following a group of subjects along as they grew older. In those earlier "cross-sectional" studies the effects of aging were distorted because the older subjects scored less well than the younger participants,

Table 16 Average Scores at Assessment and Reassessment on Mental Ability and Knowledge Tests

Test	Average Score*	
	Assessment	Reassessment
School and College Ability Test		
Verbal items	45.1	49.2
Quantitative items	40.1	42.3
Total score	86.1	91.9
Critical Thinking Test	36.5	40.4
Contemporary Affairs	30.8	45.6

See Table G (Appendix) for complete data.

*(All assessment-reassessment differences are significant at the .01 level.)

having had, on the average, less education and also schooling of a different kind. More recent "longitudinal" studies that test the same persons over the years show, as do the present data, that scores continue to rise (Bayley, 1955).

The Contemporary Affairs Test is not a test of mental ability, although scores on it correlate substantially with scholastic aptitude scores. The test was intended to measure only knowledge of current events. In an earlier chapter the recruits were described as being "woefully uninformed" at the time of original assessment. By the time of reassessment they had made noteworthy gains.

ADMINISTRATIVE SKILLS

Experience on management jobs might well be expected to change administrative ability. Most management positions, even at lower levels, involve considerable paper work, such as time and production reports, payroll changes, appraisals, writing memos, and answering letters. It is not usually expected that the entry level management recruit will have much of this kind of experience at the time of employment. Some Bell System managers, in fact, questioned the logic of administering the In-Basket to new hires, even as part of a research study, on the grounds that they lacked sufficient experience to deal with it. These managers believed that experience would certainly improve performance.

The In-Basket was, of course, the assessment technique designed to reveal administrative skills. The recruit spent three hours in this exercise, tackling management problems presented through realistic written materials. He spent an additional hour being interviewed about his reasons for taking particular actions or for failing to take action. The report written about the recruit's performance served as the main basis for the assessment staff's judgment of the variables of Organizing and Planning and Decision Making. These ratings, in turn, formed the main components of the assessment factor of Administrative Skills. In addition to these judgments made by the assessment staff, other psychologists later rated each In-Basket report from both original assessment and reassessment on overall quality of performance.

No matter which of these scores or ratings are examined—the assessment staff ratings, the administrative skills factor, or the special In-Basket evaluations—the result is the same: there was no significant difference between assessment and reassessment. At least as far as the average recruit is concerned, eight years of management experience had not improved his administrative skills.

INTERPERSONAL SKILLS

Interpersonal skills were evaluated at the assessment center mainly by two group problems—the business game and the leaderless group discussion. Each exercise called for the participation of six recruits at a time.

The business game at the original assessment center was the Manufacturing Problem, described in a previous chapter. At reassessment the business game involved a simulated and much simplified stock exchange in which the assessees were to invest as partners in a mutual fund operation. The two games were approximately equal in length and appeared to be of comparable difficulty.

The original leaderless group discussion, also described earlier, was the Promotion Problem in which each assessee advocated the promotion of a different candidate. The reassessment discussion gave the assessees the roles of members of a task force charged with making plans for reorganizing the telephone business. They were required to devise their own proposal as well as to advocate it.

In addition to the ratings of performance in these two exercises, the whole assessment staff assigned ratings on 25 variables on the basis of performance throughout the entire assessment center period. Six of the variables were especially relevant to interpersonal managerial skills—Human Relations Skills, Behavior Flexibility, Perception of Threshold Social Cues, Oral Communications Skills, Likeableness, and Forcefulness. Over and above these ratings, factor analysis produced a score for overall interpersonal skills. Table 17 shows whether a statistically reliable change occurred for each rating and, if so, the direction of the change from assessment to reassessment. The table indicates that the assessors gave significantly lower ratings from assessment to reassessment on per-

Table 17   Assessment-Reassessment Differences in Various Interpersonal Skills Ratings

Measure	Difference
Business Game, assessor rating	Down**
Group Discussion, assessor rating	Down**
Human Relations Skills	Down**
Behavior Flexibility	Down**
Perception of Threshold Social Cues	No reliable change
Oral Communications Skills	Down**
Likeableness	Down*
Forcefulness	No reliable change
Interpersonal Skills	Down**

See Tables E, F, and H (Appendix) for data.

*Significant at .05 level.

**Significant at .01 level.

formance in both group exercises and on four of the six variables. The interpersonal skills factor, which is based largely on these variable ratings, also declined significantly. The assessors obviously saw the average recruit as performing less effectively interpersonally than he had done eight years previously.

Such results are surprising, to say the least. The recruits had certainly had much opportunity for group interaction during their years in the business. It would be reasonable to expect such practice to improve interpersonal skills. Furthermore, it is difficult to conceive of people losing interpersonal ability (except for cases of mental illness). It seems more likely that ability has not been lost but that manifest behavior has for some reason changed in the direction of being less effective.

OVERALL MANAGEMENT ABILITY

The importance of management ability in any study of management careers dictated special attention to this area even before the above-mentioned results were known. Two psychologists highly experienced in assessment methods were instructed to review all the reports and ratings on each assessee and to assign new general ratings. One was to be a rating of overall management ability at the time of original assessment; the other, the same rating at the time of reassessment. The two reviewers were specifically instructed to be alert to any possible shifts of rating standards on the part of the assessment staff from the first to the second assessment. It was emphasized that the reviewers were quite free, for example, to give the same rating to a recruit at both assessments, even though the staff had given a different one. Ratings were to be made on a five-point scale, with 5 being high.

This thorough review substantiated the conclusion suggested by the results previously presented—that there was no significant change in the average recruit's management ability. The average rating assigned after a review of the original assessment materials was 2.8; for reassessment the comparable figure was 2.9.

This conclusion, it must be emphasized, does not mean that eight years of experience were of no consequence or that the recruits were not managing better on their jobs. We have already noted that one aspect of management ability is the knowledge the manager has of the company, his department, and the work he manages. The assessment center made no attempt to measure such knowledge, but it is certain that such an evaluation would have revealed that great changes had taken place over the eight years. It is in respect to basic management skills that no progress seems to have occurred.

RELATIONSHIPS TO PROGRESS

The results just cited are those for the entire group of recruits. Previous chapters have shown that changes in some of the recruits' characteristics were related to success on the job. Therefore, as a next step in the analysis of any possible changes in management ability over the years of the Study, the total group of subjects was divided into those who had and those who had not made middle management by the time of reassessment. The two groups were

136 CHANGES IN MANAGEMENT ABILITIES

then compared to determine whether they had changed differentially in management ability over the eight-year period. The comparison was made on all the 21 scores, ratings, and factors previously mentioned in this chapter: five test scores, three ratings of performance in assessment exercises, nine assessment variable ratings, three assessment factors, and one special overall management ability rating. Of the 21, only three showed any significantly differential changes from assessment to reassessment for the two progress groups. These were the "personal impact" variables of Forcefulness and Likeableness and the variable called Perception of Social Cues. Table 18, which lists the average ratings at assessment and reassessment for the two groups, indicates that the recruits who had reached middle management by the time of reassessment had changed little on these variables. The small changes shown were not nearly statistically reliable. The remainder of the recruits—those who had not reached middle management— exhibited downward changes that were statistically significant. The drop was particularly sharp in the case of Likeableness. The less successful recruits had apparently become less pleasant and tactful in group and social situations.

Table 18   Assessment Staff Ratings of Three Interpersonal
Variables for Those Who Did and Did Not Reach Middle Management

		Average Rating	
Variable	Management Level	Assess-ment	Reassess-ment
Forcefulness	Middle management	2.9	3.0
	Below middle management	2.7	2.5
Likeableness	Middle management	3.0	2.9
	Below middle management	3.0	2.5
Perception of Threshold Social Cues	Middle management	3.2	3.3
	Below middle management	2.9	2.6

See Table L (Appendix) for complete data.

To determine more exactly just which group of recruits was responsible for the decline in ratings on interpersonal skills, the total group was divided, as in the previous chapter, into four categories: the "true positives" (those who were predicted to reach middle management and did reach it), the "false positives" (those who were predicted to reach middle management and did not reach it), and, analogously, the "true negatives" and the 'false negatives." Once again changes from assessment to reassessment on the 21 management ability scores and ratings were compared. Once again, also, no significant differences in amount of change appeared in respect to the administrative skills dimensions.

However, a number of significant differences were revealed in the interpersonal skills ratings (see Table 19). Of the nine ratings and factors, seven displayed significant differences in assessment-reassessment change, and in the two nonsignificant instances the direction of the changes paralleled those for the seven discrepant dimensions.

The dominant trend of the differential changes is quite clear. The true positives and the true negatives retained their highest and lowest positions, although both declined slightly in average ratings. A strong contrast appears, however, between the false positives and the false negatives. The false positives show the largest drop of the four groups on all nine ratings; the false negatives, on the other hand, were the only group to show higher ratings. The contrast between the two groups is sharpest on the interpersonal skills score which, it will be remembered, is a factor score including all the relevant variables. On this score the false positives showed a sharp drop from assessment to reassessment, while the false negatives managed a small gain.

Before affirming the conclusion that lack of success where success is predicted is associated with a decline in interpersonal effectiveness, the possibility of contamination in the data must be considered. The reassessment staff knew the management level of each recruit at the time of reassessment, since it was routinely included in the report of the personal interview. It is conceivable that this knowledge might have influenced the ratings given the assessees on the Management Progress Study variables. The possibility can be somewhat discounted, however, since no similar

Table 19 Assessment-Reassessment Difference in Interpersonal Skills Ratings for Four Prediction Groups

Measure	True Positives			False Positives			False Negatives			True Negatives			Sig-nificance Level
	A	R	Diff	A	R	Diff	A	R	Diff	A	R	Diff	
Business Game, assessor rating	3.7	3.0	-0.7	3.8	2.9	-0.9	3.2	2.6	-0.6	2.9	2.5	-0.4	NS
Group Discussion, assessor rating													
rating	3.9	3.0	-0.9	3.9	2.4	-1.5	3.0	2.6	-0.4	2.6	2.3	-0.3	.01
Human Relations Skills	3.4	3.0	-0.4	3.1	2.2	-0.9	2.4	2.5	+0.1	2.2	1.9	-0.3	.01
Behavior Flexibility	3.6	2.8	-0.8	3.5	2.5	-1.0	2.4	2.6	+0.2	2.5	2.1	-0.4	.01
Perception of Threshold													
Social Cues	3.5	3.4	-0.1	3.5	2.8	-0.7	2.5	3.0	+0.5	2.6	2.5	-0.1	.01
Oral Communications Skills	3.7	3.2	-0.5	3.5	2.7	-0.8	3.0	3.1	+0.1	2.6	2.5	-0.1	.05
Likeableness	3.2	3.0	-0.2	3.9	3.0	-0.9	2.7	2.8	+0.1	2.8	2.3	-0.5	NS
Forcefulness	3.1	3.1	0.0	3.5	2.5	-1.0	2.3	2.6	+0.3	2.3	2.3	0.0	.01
Interpersonal Skills	10.1	8.4	-1.7	10.0	6.8	-3.2	6.9	7.6	+0.7	7.0	6.1	-0.9	.01

See Table M (Appendix) for complete data.

effect was noted in the case of ratings of the administrative skills variables. There is no apparent reason for the staff to be influenced by knowledge of management level attained in respect to interpersonal skills but not administrative skills.

Fortunately, however, there is even stronger evidence against the possibility of contaminated ratings. At the time of original assessment, the staff made a final rating not only of "will make middle management within ten years" (the rating used in the analyses so far), but also a "should make middle management" rating. The second rating was included because the staff felt that some of the recruits might well reach middle management for some extraneous reason, such as appearance, even though they did not really have good management ability. Conversely, some others might fail to advance even though they had good ability. The "should" rating was therefore intended to be a rating of management quality. A parallel "should" rating was made at reassessment.

Table 20 gives the percentage of each of the four prediction groups rated as "should make middle management" at assessment and at reassessment. The group of particular interest at the moment is the false positive group. Significantly, although there was a small decrease in the percentage of this group seen as truly having middle management ability, nearly half received the same high rating. It seems most improbable, therefore, that the lower ratings

Table 20   Percentage of Four Prediction Groups Rated as "Should Make Middle Management" at Assessment and Reassessment

Group	N	"Should Make Middle Management" (%)	
		Assessment	Reassessment
True positives	39	77	67
False positives	22	59	45
False negatives	20	10	60
True negatives	42	2	24
Total	123	37%	47%

of this group on interpersonal skills were due to a biasing of the staff ratings of the variables.

The most noteworthy aspect of Table 20 is the large jump in the percentage of the false negatives who were seen as truly having middle management ability. Once again the possibility of influence on the ratings comes to mind, but it should be noted that 36 percent of all the recruits who had reached middle management were rated "should *not* be middle management" (true positives and false negatives combined).

The average score on the interpersonal skills factor was 8.5 at assessment and 7.2 at reassessment. Thus one other aspect of the ratings should be considered—it is possible that the reassessment staffs were somewhat more stringent in judging interpersonal skills than the original assessment staffs had been eight years earlier. Assuming this to be true and assuming that the average score should have been the same at assessment and reassessment, the factor scores of the four prediction groups could be adjusted upward by 1.3. The results of doing this are shown in Table 21. Changes for those who had fared as predicted—the true positives and the true negatives—were small and insignificant. Those whose progress was different from prediction did change significantly in opposite directions. As before, the false negatives gained and the false positives lost.

Table 21   Assessment-Reassessment Change on Interpersonal Skills Factor for Four Prediction Groups

| | | Interpersonal Skills Factor | | |
| | | | Reassessment | |
Group	N	Assessment	(Adjusted)	Difference
True positives	39	10.1	9.7	−0.4
False positives	22	10.0	8.1	−1.9
False negatives	20	6.9	8.9	+2.0
True negatives	42	7.0	7.4	+0.4
Total	123	8.5	8.5	—

The foregoing analyses make it clear that a change occurred in the effectiveness of interpersonal behavior of two groups of recruits over the eight-year period. Since it is difficult to believe that interpersonal ability declines, it would seem that the less effective behavior of the false positives is due to a change in motivation. Many of this group of recruits looked very promising not only at assessment but at reassessment, as well, yet their advancement has been slow. It is reasonable to believe that frustration at not moving ahead in accordance with their capacities has caused them to be less willing to be flexible, cooperative, or even involved in group situations. Put the other way around, they may have become somewhat more hostile and self-centered.

The false negatives were definitely more interpersonally effective at reassessment. We cannot say whether this represents a real change in ability or whether it is more a change in the personality-motivational area. It is possible that advancement into middle management allowed, even required, the recruits in this group to practice interpersonal behavior in groups (e.g., in interdepartmental meetings and task forces). Their ability might thus have been developed. On the other hand, perhaps rapid advancement has acted to increase their self-confidence, and an ability that was already present has come forth.

SUMMARY REMARKS

Organizations are necessarily concerned with the underlying abilities of their managers. Much thought and effort go into attempts to maximize such talents by a variety of selection and development procedures. Earlier chapters have demonstrated that it is possible to evaluate management ability with much more accuracy than is usually provided by assessments made at the time of employment. This chapter has examined the effects of the first eight years of management experience, often thought of as a time of most important growth in such abilities.

The startling general finding is that there was no change in overall management ability for the average recruit. If those who recruited and assigned the subjects in the Management Progress

Study expected that early experience would develop most of the recruits significantly, they were certainly wrong.

Hidden within this general finding, however, are some results of interest. One is that mental ability continued to grow during the early years of adulthood. Since no differential changes were observed between the more and less successful recruits or between those who advanced as expected and those who did not, this growth appears to be associated with growing older rather than with particular work experiences.

Another finding of interest is that the recruits became much better informed about goings on in the world. Evidently, they read newspapers and news magazines, attended to news broadcasts, and discussed current events more regularly than they had while in college. No doubt they would have shown an even more impressive gain in knowledge, had they been tested on information about the telephone company operations and their particular part of them.

Also unchanged, on the average, were administrative skills for all recruits—for those who were more or less successful, or for those whose predicted success matched or did not match what actually happened. Since the predictive analysis reported in an earlier chapter showed ratings on administrative skills to be strongly related to advancement, this finding is significant. It would seem that administrative skills ought to be subject to development. If so, we will require more deliberate attempts to foster such abilities than merely letting managers manage.

The general finding for all recruits was that interpersonal skills declined. Assuming that the assessment staffs were judging this area equally stringently at assessment and reassessment, this result apparently represents not a loss in ability but perhaps a lesser concern for group harmony as one goes through the early adult years. This possibility is consistent with some of the changes on self-report personality questionnaires, reported in the following chapter.

Whether the total group declined in the effectiveness of their interpersonal behavior or stayed about the same, however, two groups of recruits clearly changed relative to one another—the false positives and the false negatives.

10

Walter Katkovsky

CHANGES IN MOTIVATION, PERSONALITY, AND JOB ATTITUDES

During the first eight years of the Study the lives of the recruits developed as they grew older. Many who had been bachelors got married, and they and the others who had preceded them to the altar became fathers and homeowners and grew accustomed to being the employees of a large corporation. As has been seen, their life styles changed, sometimes quite dramatically. An important question is, were these changes simply modifications of behavior as the recruits adjusted to the realities and demands of their lives, or did they reflect—or cause—deeper changes in motivation and personality? The data examined in this chapter deal with changes in the men between assessment and reassessment in various measures that pertain to motivation and personality, as well as to the attitudes of the men about their jobs and careers. Changes in the total group are discussed first, followed by comparisons of the changes in the more successful group with the less successful group.

MOTIVATION AND PERSONALITY

Four of the seven factors underlying the assessment variables represent motivational or personality characteristics. They are

Work Motivation, Career Orientation, Stability of Performance, and Independence of Others (the other three factors concerning management ability were discussed in the preceding chapter). In the first part of this chapter we consider changes in these four motivational areas from assessment to reassessment.

The motivational factors were derived primarily from ten of the Management Progress Study variables rated by the assessment staff. Before making these ratings, it will be recalled, the assessment staff listened to reports on all the assessment techniques. The techniques particularly relevant to the motivational dimensions were of two general kinds. The interview and the projective tests were of one type. The interview covered a wide range of topics, including educational and occupational background, family relationships, goals and aspirations, the nature of and reactions to job assignments, and characteristics of the interpersonal situation on the job. In the projective tests, the subjects were asked to respond to relatively unstructured materials with their personal perceptions and feelings. Ratings of the subjects' responses involved analysis, interpretation, and judgments by the assessment staff or coders of the tests and reports. The other type of technique was the questionnaire, specifically the Edwards Personal Preference Schedule and the Guilford-Martin Inventory of Factors (GAMIN).* On these the subject described himself by selecting statements which best characterized his likes, dislikes, or his usual behavior as he saw it. These answers were scored mechanically and the scores represented the subject's self-perceptions on a variety of motivational and personality dimensions.

At the assessment center a separate report was prepared and presented to the staff on the interview data, as well as yet another report on the subject's responses to the projective tests. These narrative reports presented a general description of the subject's background, personality, goals, and aspirations, with emphasis on characteristics that might influence his management career. These reports were not rated separately at the assessment center, but they were quantified for research purposes some years later. A

---

* Published respectively by the Psychological Corporation, New York, N.Y. and the Sheridan Supply Company, Beverly Hills, Calif.

team of graduate students in psychology was trained, and its members rated every assessment and reassessment interview and projective report on a number of variables.

Three kinds of data, therefore, were available on motivational and personality dimensions—the special ratings of the interviews and projective tests, the scores on the questionnaires, and the ratings of Management Progress variables made by the assessment staffs. There were more than 50 scores and ratings that might be considered. In the interest of orderly presentation, the ratings and scores that are substantially related to the four motivational factors listed previously form the core of the discussion.

The ratings and scores under each factor were identified in the following manner: ratings of the interview or projective test reports, or any questionnaire score, which correlated .30 or more with a factor were included under that factor. Also included were the assessment staff ratings shown to be involved in the factor by the factor analysis reported in Chapter 7.

CHANGES FOR THE TOTAL GROUP

The factor called Work Motivation includes the assessment variable ratings of Primacy of Work and Inner Work Standards. In addition, three of the special ratings were substantially related to this factor—the ratings of the interview reports for Primacy of Work and Inner Work Standards and the ratings of the projective test reports for Work Orientation. Only one of these five ratings showed a significant change from assessment to reassessment, namely, the rating of Inner Work Standards from the interview report. It should be emphasized that the assessment staff's rating of this variable, considering all the assessment reports, changed hardly at all from assessment to reassessment. Neither did the assessment factor itself change. These results are presented in Table 22.

The factor of Career Orientation includes the assessment variable ratings of Need Advancement, Ability to Delay Gratification (negative), and Need Security (negative). Related to this factor were two of the special ratings of the interview—Need Advance-

Table 22   Assessment-Reassessment Changes in Work Motivation Factor and Associated Measures

Measure	Source	Change*
Work Motivation	Factor	—
Primacy of Work	Variable	—
Inner Work Standards	Variable	—
Primacy of Work	Interview	—
Inner Work Standards	Interview	Increase
Work Orientation	Projective tests	—

See Tables E, F, J, and K (Appendix) for data.

* Indicated changes significant at the .05 level or better; no entry indicates change not significant at that level.

ment and Need Security (negative)—and five of the special ratings on the projective tests—Self-Confidence, Leadership Role, Dependence (negative), Subordinate Role (negative), and Achievement Motivation. In addition, two scores from the Guilford-Martin Inventory were related—those for General Activity and Ascendancy. There were thus twelve ratings and scores in all (see Table 23). Of these, the Table indicates three significant changes from assessment to reassessment, as follows: a decrease in the rating of Need Advancement from the interview, an increase in the rating of Self-Confidence from the projective tests, and a decrease in the Ascendancy score on the Guilford-Martin Inventory. Once again, the assessment staff ratings did not change significantly, nor did the assessment factor itself.

The factor Stability of Performance includes the assessment variable ratings of Resistance to Stress and Tolerance of Uncertainty. Only one of the other scores or ratings—the interview rating of Tolerance of Uncertainty—was associated with this factor. Over the eight years of the study, one assessment variable rating changed significantly—there was a decrease in Tolerance of Uncertainty. In this case, the assessment factor itself also dropped significantly (see Table 24).

Table 23   Assessment-Reassessment Change in Career
Orientation Factor and Associated Measures

Measure	Source	Change*
Career Orientation	Factor	—
Need Advancement	Variable	—
Ability to Delay Gratifi-cation	Variable	—
Need Security	Variable	—
Need Advancement	Interview	Decrease
Need Security	Interview	—
Self-Confidence	Projective tests	Increase
Leadership Role	Projective tests	—
Dependence	Projective tests	—
Subordinate Role	Projective tests	—
Achievement Motivation	Projective tests	—
General Activity	Guilford-Martin Inventory	—
Ascendancy	Guilford-Martin Inventory	Decrease

See Tables E, F, I, J, and K (Appendix) for data.

* Indicated changes significant at the .05 level or better; no entry
indicates change not significant at that level.

Table 24   Assessment-Reassessment Changes in Stability of Performance Factor and Associated Measures

Measure	Source	Change*
Stability of Performance	Factor	Decrease
Resistance to Stress	Variable	—
Tolerance of Uncertainty	Variable	Decrease
Tolerance of Uncertainty	Interview	—

See Tables E, F, and K (Appendix) for data.

* Indicated changes significant at the .05 level or better;
no entry indicates change not significant at that level.

The factor Independence of Others includes the three assessment variable ratings of Need Approval of Superiors (negative), Need Approval of Peers (negative), and Goal Flexibility (negative). Five ratings made on the basis of the projective test reports correlate with this factor: Self-Confidence, Affiliation (negative), Leadership Role, Dependence (negative), and Subordinate Role (negative). All three assessment variable ratings dropped significantly from assessment to reassessment; that is, the recruits were seen as more independent and more fixed or stable in their career goals. In addition, the projective test ratings of Self-Confidence and Affiliation also moved in a more confident and independent direction. The assessment factor itself increased significantly. Results are given in Table 25.

In addition to the changes in the ratings and scores associated with the assessment factors, certain other statistically significant differences between assessment and reassessment were observed. These data are presented in Table 26. Most of the changes fit in well with the results reported under the various assessment factors. The decline in Need Approval of Superiors as judged from the interview reports is obviously consistent with the changes noted

Table 25 Assessment-Reassessment Changes in Independence of Others Factor and Associated Measures

Measure	Source	Change*
Independence of Others	Factor	Increase
Need Approval of Superiors	Variable	Decrease
Need Approval of Peers	Variable	Decrease
Goal Flexibility	Variable	Decrease
Self-Confidence	Projectives	Increase
Affiliation	Projectives	Decrease
Leadership Role	Projectives	—
Dependence	Projectives	—
Subordinate Role	Projectives	—

See Tables E, F, and J (Appendix) for data.

* Indicated changes significant at the .05 level or better; no entry indicates change not significant at that level.

Table 26   Additional Assessment-Reassessment Changes

Measure	Source	Change*
Need Approval of Superiors	Interview	Decrease
Need Achievement	Edwards	Increase
Need Autonomy	Edwards	Increase
Need Dominance	Edwards	Increase
Need Aggression	Edwards	Increase
Need Deference	Edwards	Decrease
Need Affiliation	Edwards	Decrease
Need Abasement	Edwards	Decrease
Self-Confidence	Guilford-Martin	Decrease

See Tables I and K (Appendix) for data.

* Changes significant at .05 level or better.

under the Independence of Others factor. The same is true of the changes in scores on the Edwards Personal Preference Schedule, particularly the increases in Need Autonomy, Need Dominance, and Need Aggression, and decreases in Need Deference, Need Affiliation, and Need Abasement. The following list indicates the type of items* making up each of these scores:

Achievement. To do one's best, to be successful, to do a difficult job well, to be able to do things better than others.

Autonomy. To be able to come and go as desired, to be independent of others in making decisions, to feel free to do what one wants, to do things without regard to what others may think.

Dominance. To argue for one's point of view, to be a leader in groups to which one belongs, to be elected or appointed chairman of committees, to supervise and direct the action of others.

* Excerpted from the *Manual for the Edwards Personal Preference Schedule,* Copyright 1954, © 1959 by the Psychological Corporation, New York, N.Y.

Aggression. To attack contrary points of view, to tell others what one thinks of them, to tell others off when disagreeing with them, to criticize others publicly.

Deference. To follow instructions and do what is expected, to accept the leadership of others, to let others make decisions, to conform to custom and avoid the unconventional.

Affiliation. To participate in friendly groups, to do things with friends rather than alone, to form new friendships, to make as many friends as possible.

Abasement. To accept blame when things do not go right, to feel depressed by inability to handle situations, to feel inferior to others in most respects, to feel guilty when one does something wrong.

Another finding of interest is the rise in the general adjustment ratings. One of these was the rating made from the overall projective test report; the other was the rating arrived at solely on the basis of the subject's responses on the Rotter Incomplete Sentences Blank. On the Rotter test, subjects are asked to complete sentences in a way that expresses their "real feelings," and the responses are scored for indications of maladjustment in accordance with a manual provided by the author of the test.

The decline in the Self-Confidence score on the Guilford-Martin Inventory is definitely inconsistent with the other data, and no precise explanation is available. It is possible that the inconsistency is attributable to differences in the measurement methods. That is, the drop in self-confidence on the inventory may indicate that the subjects gave more realistic and honest reports of their self-doubts than they had provided eight years earlier, when many of them could be described as naïvely positive in their self-appraisals. In contrast, the other adjustment and confidence measures involved the staff's impressions and took into account factors other than the subjects' expressed self-confidence, such as personal conflicts and frustrations. Based on the latter ratings, the men appeared to be better adjusted at the time of the reassessment than at the initial assessment.

What can be said, then, about the average recruit? The general findings were that the average recruit was better adjusted and more independent after eight years more of life than he had been when he entered the business. He was, for example, less interested in getting approval from others, more self-confident, and less likely to change his goals in accordance with outside pressures. It seems likely that such changes were the result of both on-the-job and off-the-job experiences. Although many of the recruits had not advanced as rapidly as they might have hoped, all had certainly proved capable of doing a management-level job in a prestigious corporation. The demands of their management jobs probably encouraged the increases in autonomy and confidence. Furthermore, since the general tone of their respective careers was quite well set, they did not have to be as acutely concerned with what others thought of them. On the outside, the great majority had wives and children and might therefore be expected to look less to business associates for interpersonal satisfaction. Their personal lives, as well as their careers, were more stable and secure, and all the subjects were living in a comfortable, middle-class style. Most had successfully assumed the typical responsibilities of husband and parent, and this undoubtedly contributed to the improvement in overall adjustment noted in the changes.

RELATIONSHIPS TO PROGRESS

In previous chapters some changes between assessment and reassessment were found to be related to advancement in management. A next step, therefore, was to examine changes in the personality-motivational measures against progress.

In the previous section we considered 28 ratings and scores associated with the four personality-motivational assessment factors. When changes in these 32 measures were compared for the recruits who had reached middle management by the time of reassessment and those who had not, only two significant differences were found. These were on the assessment variables of Primacy of Work and Goal Flexibility. The recruits who had reached middle management by the time of reassessment showed a substantial gain in Primacy of Work over the eight-year period, whereas the less successful recruits displayed a loss. Both groups declined from assessment to reassessment in Goal Flexibility, but the less successful men evidenced a significantly sharper drop. At the time of original assessment the men who were to be less successful showed considerably more Goal Flexibility than the others. At reassessment, both groups were at the same level.

Several other differences in scores and ratings not highly associated with the assessment factors are worth mentioning. Two of these were the assessment staff rating of Bell System Value Orientation and the rating of Work Orientation from the projective test reports. In both instances the recruits who had reached middle management had risen on these dimensions, while the less successful had declined. These results fit in nicely with the parallel changes for Primacy of Work just noted. It is clear and quite logical that those who were more successful were becoming more involved in their work and more enthusiastic about the Bell System than those who were doing less well.

Only the Need Abasement score on the Edwards Personal Preference Schedule showed a significantly differential change for the successful and less successful groups. We have seen that the average score for all recruits declined from assessment to reassessment; the present analysis traced this decline to a sharp drop for the men who had not reached middle management. These recruits report themselves as less likely to accept blame when things do not go right and less likely to feel inferior or to be depressed by inability to handle situations. They seem to be saying, "I'm not doing as well as might have been expected, but I'm not taking the blame!"

Once again, some of the results from the Guilford-Martin Inventory are difficult to explain. The successful men changed differently from the less successful in scores from the Guilford-Martin questionnaire on Self-Confidence and Masculinity. Although the less successful group remained stable in Self-Confidence and scored higher in Masculinity, the more successful group decreased on the same measures. These differential changes may indicate that the more successful group had experienced a more realistic awareness of self-doubts and a broadening of interests beyond culturally

The first year after assessment they were asked to predict four years ahead, the next year three years ahead, and so forth, until five years following the assessment, when they were supposed to respond as they saw things currently. During the remaining years until reassessment, they also responded as they saw things at the time they were completing the inventory.

An additional requirement at each administration was that the managers indicate the items that were most important to them. Table 28 gives assessment and reassessment endorsement of four inventory items originally reported as having great importance to the recruits. Three of them concern job challenge and opportunity. The other indicates regret at having taken a job with the telephone company. Although all items showed some decline in the favorability of response, the change was dramatic for only one of them. Whereas originally 88 percent thought they would be advanced as rapidly as their interests and abilities warranted, less than half believed that this was likely at the reassessment. The change would seem to be an almost automatic result, since only 37

Table 28   Percentage Responding Favorably to Four Expectation Items at Assessment and Seven Years Later

Item	Percentage with Favorable Expectation at Original Assessment	Percentage with Favorable View Seven Years Later
I am advanced about as rapidly as my interest and ability warrant.	88	47
I have a real chance to follow my basic interests and work at the things I like to do.	95	77
My job is challenging with many opportunities to learn and do new things.	98	82
I regret not having gone to work for another company.	99	84

percent of the recruits had reached middle management levels by reassessment.

The other three items in the table showed lesser declines. It is noteworthy that although the majority of recruits were working at levels below middle management, 82 percent said that their jobs were challenging. In this connection it might be recalled that independent raters had judged that only 38 percent of the recruits had experienced high job challenge. It may be that some of this seeming overestimation of job challenge on the part of the subjects is self-protective. One's self-esteem may suffer from an admission that one is staying on an undemanding job. On the other hand, the relations between a person's abilities and his job and his own definition of challenging work may result in judgments different from those rating jobs in the abstract. Even so, one-sixth of the recruits were willing to concede that they wished they had gone to work elsewhere.

A rough scoring method for the Expectations Inventory was developed as a general indicator of the favorability of expectations. Instructions for the Inventory called for the subject to respond on a scale ranging from +2 (fairly certain to be true) to —2 (fairly certain to be false), depending on his expectations. A score was computed for the 28 favorable items on the blank by adding the responses on these items. The total score thus could run from +56 to —56.

Original expectations were highly favorable, with the average score being 26.0; eight years later, the average was 9.4. Annual scores for these and the intervening years are charted in Figure 14. Trends are presented separately for the recruits who were in middle management at reassessment and for those who were not. Although both the more successful and the less successful recruits evidenced an early decline in expectations, the more successful group not only showed a lesser decline but a sharp upturn at the time of reassessment. As might be expected, the degree to which the recruits looked on various aspects of their work life as favorable was influenced by the progress they had made. There was a correlation of .51 at reassessment between management level and favorability of expectations.

The marked decline in expectations does not necessarily indicate that recruits had encountered highly negative job situations or

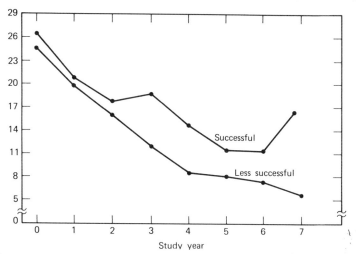

Figure 14   Average Expectations Inventory Score for the Successful and
Less Successful Groups, by Year. See Table P (Appendix)
for data.

dissatisfaction with their careers. In most cases the drop is more
indicative of changes in the idealistic and naïve views held by many
of the recruits at the time of employment. As the years passed,
they became more realistic about life, themselves, and their
opportunities, and these changes were reflected in less positive
outlooks concerning their careers.

Starting the first year after assessment and continuing annually
thereafter, the recruits filled out a Management Attitude Survey,
which was a specially constructed instrument used with middle
management throughout the Bell System in the 1950s. This survey
questionnaire yielded scores on a number of scales, several of
which are of interest. The most global scale was that of "general
management attitude," which referred to the overall feeling about
the telephone company. A sample item from that scale read:

How much pride would you say you take in working for
the Company?
None at all.
Some, but not much.
Quite a bit.
A great deal.

The trend of the average general management attitude score for all recruits over the seven annual administrations of the Survey appears in Figure 15, along with the trends for those who had reached middle management by the time of reassessment and those who had not. Once again, as with the Expectations Inventory, the general trend is downward from originally highly positive attitudes. The differences between the more successful and the less successful groups start earlier and are more consistent than was the case with the Expectations Inventory. Those who were to make middle management within eight years had more favorable attitudes even at the first administration (one year after the first assessment) and declined much more gradually.

The trends on the personal satisfaction Survey scale are plotted in Figure 16. This scale concerns such variables as opportunities for advancement and amount of responsibility. For the group as a whole there is an early decline and then a rise, with the average score at the reassessment about where it started. (This is the only scale on which the final average score is not definitely below the initial score.) There is, however, a very clear difference between

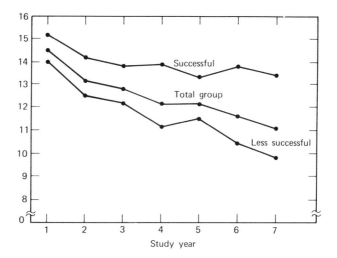

Figure 15   Average General Management Attitude Score each Year after Assessment for Successful, Less Successful, and Total Groups. See Table P (Appendix) for data.

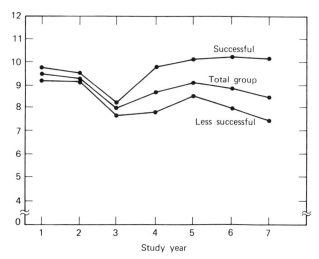

Figure 16   Average Personal Satisfaction Score each Year after Assessment for Successful, Less Successful, and Total Groups. See Table P (Appendix) for Data.

those who reached middle management and those who did not. Although the two groups are quite similar for three years after initial assessment, they separate decisively after that.

The job satisfaction scale, which concerns day-to-day reactions to the job, elicited rather different results. The general trend is gradually downward, as Figure 17 reveals; but except for a sharp rise at the third administration of the Survey, the more successful group is less different from the less successful group than would be expected.

The items on the personal satisfaction scale have to do with opportunities to get ahead, fairness of promotions, amount of responsibility given to an individual, and freedom to use one's own judgment. It is not surprising that those who had risen further in the company answered more positively. The job satisfaction scale items on which there was much less difference between the groups were as follows:

Are there any things about your job that you particularly dislike?

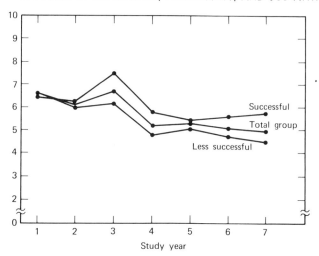

Figure 17   Average Job Satisfaction Score each Year after Assessment for Successful, Less Successful, and Total Groups. See Table P (Appendix) for data.

How often do you look forward with some pleasure to your day on the job?

If someone asked you about getting a job with the Telephone Company, which of the following would you be inclined to do? (Encourage it; Discourage it; Neither encourage it nor discourage it.)

Do you regret having gone to work for the Telephone Company?

Do you ever feel that you would like to quit and get a job with some other company?

The dissimilarities in group trends between the personal satisfaction and the job satisfaction scales appear to be due to the differences in the items, although both sets of items refer to the job. Those in the personal satisfaction scale relate to degree of responsibility, opportunities for advancement, and other factors more likely to characterize middle management jobs. Items in the job satisfaction scale are more concerned with the day-to-day pleasantness of the job, and here there is much less difference between the middle management group and those who had not advanced beyond the second level. That the two scales are not highly related is seen in the correlation between them—namely, .51.

Several analyses were performed in an effort to illuminate the determinants of attitudes held by the recruits. These analyses were based on the general management attitude score. One immediate finding was that the general attitude score was only of medium stability. Scores from one year to the next correlated approximately .55. This indicates that the recruits cannot be thought of as having formed a view of the company which remained stable from one year to the next. It has been seen that general management attitudes declined from year to year. Within that decline, the recruits changed their relative general positions considerably.

It appears that more than the initial year in the company is required for a stable general attitude to be established. Table 29, which lists the correlations between general management attitude scores for the several years of administration, reveals that the coefficients between the first administration and the later ones are

Table 29 Correlations between General Management Attitude Scores for Seven Annual Administrations*

	Study Year						
Study Year	1	2	3	4	5	6	7
1	—	51	27	26	29	16	24
2		—	53	52	42	39	45
3			—	55	49	45	46
4				—	58	56	50
5					—	53	55
6						—	58
7							—

* $p < .05$ for $r > .17$.

Table 30   Selected Correlations with General Management
Attitude at Study Year 7*

Variable	Correlation with General Management Attitude at Year 7
General management attitude at year 4	.50
Management level at year 7	.31
Overall job challenge for seven years	.13

* $p < .05$ for $r > .17$.

quite low (except for the immediately following year). The second
administration, two years after assessment, indicates considerably
higher relationships with the later years.

In line with analyses made on other data, it is important to
determine whether general management attitude is significantly
related to the level of management achieved or to the ratings of
job challenge. Table 30 presents selected relationships pertinent
to this question. There is a significant relationship of .31 between
level at year 7 and general management attitude score the same
year. Scores at year 7, however, are predicted better by scores at
year 4 (.50) than by level at year 7. Job challenge experienced over
the seven years is not significantly related to this attitude score.

SUMMARY REMARKS

What are the most general findings that emerge from this array
of personality, motivational, and attitudinal data? It is clear that
the total group of recruits became more realistic—or, one might
say, less idealistic—about life in a business enterprise and about
their individual careers. As this was happening, they were developing patterns of motivation more typical of managers. They were
decidedly less dependent on others, more achievement oriented,
more interested in influencing others, more aggressive, and less
interested in affiliating with and deferring to others.

A corollary finding is that the recruits appeared to be better
adjusted and, based on the judgments of others, more self-confident.

It is noteworthy, on the other hand, that little indication exists that they became any more work motivated or any more motivated for advancement than they had been before they had acquired eight years of telephone company experience.

When the total group of recruits is divided into various progress groups, some additional findings are revealed. There are indications that those who advanced more rapidly became more involved in work than those who did not. There is considerable evidence that, as certainly would be expected, the more successful group retained the more favorable attitudes to their jobs and to their employer. Finally, the recruits who did not do as well as predicted dropped off on some aspects of job motivation, whereas those who did better than predicted showed a rise on many of the same dimensions.

The movement of the total group of recruits toward more independence and better adjustment was *not* related to advancement. It appears that these important changes are associated more with the progress made by both groups in developing stable and secure life styles than with the specific level of job success experienced.

11

THOSE WHO LEFT

The recruiting and employment of college graduates is a costly undertaking. There is first of all the expense involved in the whole employment apparatus, including campus visits, interviewing and testing, and visits to the company by the more promising applicants. An additional heavy cost is incurred in the salaries and training expenditures for those who are hired but leave the employing organization early in their careers. Most businesses can expect to lose at least half those hired.

It was expected at the outset of the Management Progress Study that half the college recruits taken into the Study would eventually leave and that about 40 percent would leave within ten years from the time of original assessment. These expectations, based on previous Bell System experience, proved to be quite accurate. By the time of reassessment eight years later, 38 percent of the recruits were no longer System employees. (This figure and the remaining data used in this chapter exclude the three subjects who died prior to reassessment.) The men in the Study proved, once again, to be quite representative of Bell System recruits generally.

FORCED AND VOLUNTARY TERMINATION

The official records of businesses often show that the great majority of college recruits who terminate do so voluntarily and that their work is satisfactory while they are on the payroll. The implication is that organizations are losing a disproportionate amount of valuable talent. In the Bell System, termination data indicated that 80 percent of the management hire terminations were voluntary.

The confidential interviews conducted as part of the Study with the recruits who left and with their final supervisor suggested that a correction of the official figures was in order. Only about half the terminations were completely voluntary; the others were to various degrees forced. In some cases the pressure was mild. The boss might simply answer a question about possible promotion in the negative, also seconding the recruit's response that "Maybe I'd better try someplace else before it's too late." In other instances more heat was generated, and the departure was more of the "you-can't-fire-me-I-quit" variety.

Nearly all the involuntary terminators were let go because of poor job performance or because they were judged not to have potential for advancement. (It will be recalled that the recruits were employed on the premise that they had middle management ability.) Only a very few were dismissed for other reasons such as insubordination or dishonesty. The emphasis on promotability appears to have varied substantially among departments. Table 31 gives the voluntary and forced termination rates by department. Engineering and Accounting show very low forced termination rates—4 and 9 percent, respectively. These departments have more nonsupervisory "production" jobs at lower management levels than the other departments. They are thus willing to retain college graduates with low managerial ability as long as they perform their assigned tasks satisfactorily.

The interviews with the voluntary terminators conducted soon after they left the company were carefully reviewed in an effort to determine why each recruit had chosen to resign. The stated reasons fell into a few major categories (see Table 32). The number of reasons is larger than the number of separatees because some of the men gave more than one reason for leaving.

Uninteresting or unchallenging work and lack of opportunity were by far the most frequently mentioned reasons. (The "other" category included, among other things, the large size of the company and poor supervision.) Although there is no doubt that the reasons given reflect legitimate complaints, caution is advisable

Table 31 Terminations Eight Years After Assessment, by Department

Original Department	Number of Recruits				Percentages Terminated		
	Original Group	Forced Terminators	Voluntary Terminators	Total Terminators	Forced Terminators	Voluntary Terminators	Total Terminators
Plant	62	18	12	30	29	19	48
Commercial	58	14	12	26	24	21	45
Traffic	51	8	11	19	16	21	37
Engineering	55	2	7	9	4	13	16
Accounting	33	3	6	9	9	18	27
Other	12	7	4	11	58	33	92
Total	271	52	52	104	19%	19%	38%

Table 32   Reasons for Leaving the Company Given by the
52 Voluntary Terminators

Reason	Number Mentioning	Percentage Mentioning
Uninteresting or unchallenging work	29	56
Lack of opportunity	22	42
Home–personal	10	19
Military service	5	10
Other	9	17
Total	75	144%

in accepting these results as complete explanations of why voluntary terminations took place. The interviewers often received the impression that a terminator did not really know the basic reason for his decision, even though he could readily give socially desirable and apparently logical answers.

The Bell System lost the services of approximately two out of five of the original group of recruits within the first eight years of employment. This is the quantitative finding. What about the quality of those who remained as compared with the original total group? The upper two bars in Figure 18 show the percentage of the original and remainder groups judged to have middle management potential at the time of original assessment. These percentages are almost identical.

In terms of potential to reach the third level of management (the assessment standard), separations did not change the balance of talent in the college recruits on the payroll. The reason for this result appears in the lower two bars of Figure 18. Although the voluntary leavers showed higher potential than those who stayed, those forced out were of lower potential to a comparable degree. Since the voluntary and forced groups were of the same size, the two types of departure canceled each other out qualitatively.

A closer examination of the potential ratings, however, revealed an unexpectedly dramatic finding. The assessment staff had rated 10 percent of the original group of recruits (27 men) as having

Assessment rating: "should be middle management"

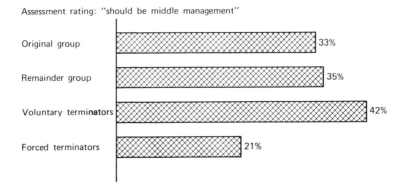

Figure 18   Effect of Terminations on Quality of Management Group.

greater than third level potential. In the eyes of the assessors, these were the cream of the college hires. By the time of reassessment only one of these men had left the company, and he had chosen to enter the ministry!

It is not surprising that the rate of forced termination for this top group is low, although the zero result is certainly remarkable. (The power of the assessment center in identifying such a group should not be overlooked.) What is more surprising is that voluntary termination should also be nearly absent. Part of the reason is probably that the job challenge and progress experienced by this group was greater than for the men with lesser potential—58 percent of the high-potential men had had a high degree of job challenge, as compared with 38 percent of the total group of recruits. Moreover, 58 percent of these recruits had reached middle management by the time of reassessment, as compared with 37 percent of the total group.

Yet it does not seem that the factors just enumerated could account completely for the amazing sticking power of the highly assessed men. Perhaps they are highly intrinsically motivated—this would tend to net for them higher evaluations at assessment and would also make them less likely to quit even if their job situation were not ideal.

LATER CAREERS

Termination from the company did not mean the end of participation in the Management Progress Study for the recruits. All were
interviewed shortly after leaving the business, and they were
followed up periodically thereafter by both face-to-face and telephone interviews. Their continued cooperation has been remarkable.

All the separatees had had a more or less unsatisfying experience with a large corporation, the Bell System, and it might have
been expected that they would have shunned big companies in
selecting their next employer. Actually, half the men went right
to work for another large firm, and this was true to exactly the
same degree for both the voluntary and the forced terminators. The
other half the separatees scattered to smaller employers, government, and military service, or became self-employed, or returned
to school.

The employer immediately following the Bell System was not
the last employer for many of the recruits. Half moved on at least
once more, and approximately one out of five made two or more
additional changes. These figures, of course, are only up to the
point of reassessment, when some had been away from the Bell
System only a very few years.

By the time of reassessment, after the additional moves had
occurred, there was a somewhat different pattern of employment
for the voluntary and forced terminators, as Table 33 reveals. The
forced leavers were more often found with big employers (large
corporations or the government) than the voluntary leavers—70
versus 43 percent, respectively. The voluntary leavers were more
often with a small company or self-employed—37 percent, versus
20 percent for the forced leavers. A possible explanation may be
that the voluntary leavers were, on the average, more independent
than the other separatees.

Thirty-seven percent of the recruits who stayed with the Bell
System had reached middle management by the time of reassessment. It was surprising to find that the figure for the men who had
left the company was very little different; 33 percent were in the
middle or upper management of the companies in which they were

Table 33   Employment of Terminators at the Time of Reassessment

	Percentage	
Employment	Forced Terminators (N = 52)	Voluntary Terminators (N = 52)
Large corporation	58	35
Government	12	8
Small company	6	17
Self-employed; professional	14	20
Military service	0	6
Full-time student	4	6
Other	6	8
Total	100%	100%

employed (see Table 34). However, the similarity of the figures for the two groups might be expected when it is recalled that the distribution of management potential was roughly equal in these categories. The Table also shows an expected difference between voluntary and forced leavers—43 percent of the first group had reached at least middle management, while only 25 percent of the forced terminators had done so.

The relatively large number of men in both groups of terminators who were not in management positions at all (30 and 39 percent, respectively) contrasts sharply with the recruits who had stayed in the telephone business. All those recruits were in jobs rated at management levels, although many did not have supervisory responsibilities.

Salary data also support the observation that the men who left the company spread out much more widely in their occupational status than those who stayed. Table 35 shows that 19 percent of the terminators claimed to have incomes higher than those of almost everyone still with Bell. (The reader is cautioned that the salary data for the separatees is based on the subjects' statements; the figures for the remainder group are taken from company

Table 34 Management Level Attained by Terminators
at Time of Reassessment

Management Level	Percentage		
	Voluntary Terminators (N = 30)	Forced Terminators (N = 36)	All Terminators (N = 66)
Upper	13	8	10
Middle	30	17	23
Lower	27	36	32
Nonmanagement	30	39	35
Total	100%	100%	100%

records.) On the other hand, 17 percent of the terminators report salaries less than anyone still on the company payroll.

As would be anticipated, the voluntary terminators appear to be doing substantially better than the forced leavers. Forty-seven percent of the former group report incomes in excess of $14,000, as compared with 27 percent of those whose departure from the company was not completely voluntary. Once again, the data are quite consistent with the management potential of the two groups as seen at the original assessment center.

PREDICTION OF TERMINATION

Turnover of management recruits is so costly to organizations that accurate prediction of termination would be a valuable addition to selection procedures. With this in mind, many analyses were made of information about the recruits available at the time of original assessment. Background factors investigated included age, marital status, parenthood, years of education, undergraduate major, quality of college attended, rank in college graduating class,

Table 35   Annual Salaries of Terminators and Remainder Groups at Reassessment

	Percentages			
Salary	Remainder (N = 167)	All Terminators (N = 69)	Forced Terminators (N = 37)	Voluntary Terminators (N = 32)
$16,000–up	1	19	11	28
$14,000–$15,999	11	17	16	19
$12,000–$13,999	38	17	24	9
$10,000–$11,999	38	22	19	25
$8,000–$9,999	12	22	27	16
$6,000–$7,999	0	3	3	3
Total	100%	100%	100%	100%

military service, rank at discharge from the military, and previous full-time employment.

Only one factor—marital status—was significantly related to termination; a higher proportion of the terminators were single men. Even this evidence is not easy to interpret, since it was the *forced* terminators who were responsible for the difference. The voluntary leavers were quite like those who stayed. The percentages were as follows: 39 percent of those who remained with the company and 44 percent of those who left voluntarily were single men at first assessment as compared to 60 percent of the forced terminators.

The assessment staff used the wealth of information gathered about the recruits during the three and one-half days of the original assessment to make a final judgment concerning each recruit's management potential. As we have seen, the prediction of progress in management had considerable accuracy. The staff also predicted whether the recruit would remain with the company; unfortunately, however, they did not state whether his departure, if it occurred, would be voluntary or forced. The results (see Table 36) indicate that the assessment staff was able to predict termination significant-

Table 36   Assessment Staff Prediction of Separation
from Company and Actual Separations

	N	Terminators (%)	Remainder Group (%)
Predicted to leave	83	52	48
Predicted to stay	188	32	68

Note: Difference between termination rates significant at .05 level.

	N	Forced to Terminate (%)	Terminated Voluntarily (%)
Predicted to leave	83	23	29
Predicted to stay	188	17	15

ly better than chance. Fifty-two percent of those predicted to leave did leave, compared with 32 percent of those who were not predicted to leave. The prediction was of about the same accuracy for both the voluntary and the forced groups. Although this result demonstrates that termination is not completely unpredictable, in spite of the many chance factors involved, the accuracy of the prediction is too low to be of practical use. Just about half those predicted to leave did stay.

A number of comparisons were made between the voluntary and forced termination groups. Several of these showed significant differences, such as lower mental ability test scores and poorer In-Basket performance for the forced group. The differences, however, were those that would be expected from the finding reported earlier in this chapter that only half as many of the forced as compared with the voluntary leavers were judged to have middle management potential. Such findings suggest, however, that the incidence of forced termination can be lowered by higher employment standards. Voluntary termination of college recruits does not seem to be practicably predictable at the time of initial employment.

ATTITUDES AND TERMINATION

A commonsense point of view, rarely demonstrated empirically, is that attitudes lead to behavior. If one could keep track of an employee's attitudes, it would follow that impending termination might be detected. Each recruit filled out a management attitude inventory annually, at the time of his follow-up interview. This inventory was the same instrument used for Bell System management attitude measurement throughout the 1950s. Table 37 presents the average scores on four of the scales making up the inventory for the remainder and the two terminator groups. These scores were from the first administration of the inventory, one year after first assessment.

An inspection of the table reveals that the recruits who were later to terminate voluntarily had as good or better attitudes than those who would stay with the company. Those who were destined to be asked to leave showed significantly lower attitude scores. It is likely that this group was already receiving and reacting to

Table 37   Mean Scores on Attitude Scales for Remainder and Terminator Groups One Year After Assessment

	Attitude Scales			
	General Management Attitude	Attitude toward Supervision	Personal Satisfaction	Job Satisfaction
Remainder	14.5	13.2	9.4	6.6
All terminators	13.8	12.5	8.4	5.7*
Voluntary terminators	15.6	13.8	9.4	6.3
Forced terminators	12.4*	11.5	7.5*	5.3**

See Table R (Appendix) for complete data.

* Difference from remainder group significant at .05 level.
** Difference from remainder group significant at .01 level.

negative signals about their performance. This interpretation is supported by the data in Table 38, which are the average scores for the terminators who lasted at least four years after assessment, by year, on each of the four scales. The forced terminator group was significantly lower than the other two groups beginning with the very first administration of the attitude inventory.

Interestingly, the results for the voluntary terminators reveal the attitudes of this group toward the company generally, toward supervision, and even in personal satisfaction, were as favorable for three years as those who chose to stay with the company. Only job satisfaction itself showed an early decline. During the fourth year some of the other attitude dimensions began to deteriorate. The data indicate that forced terminators develop generally poorer attitudes early in their careers. Voluntary terminators may be quite favorable in their general attitudes toward their employer until

Table 38   Means for Four Attitude Scales Through Year 5 for Remainder and Terminator Groups

Scale	Group	Years After Assessment			
		1	2	3	4
General Management	Remainder	14.5	13.2	12.8	12.2
Attitude	Voluntary	15.6	13.6	13.5	10.9
	Forced	12.4	12.3	11.1	9.1
Attitude toward	Remainder	13.2	11.5	11.1	10.2
Supervision	Voluntary	13.8	12.1	12.0	10.2
	Forced	11.5	10.3	9.6	6.3
Personal Satisfaction	Remainder	9.4	9.3	7.9	8.6
	Voluntary	9.4	9.7	8.5	7.6
	Forced	7.5	6.8	6.9	6.7
Job Satisfaction	Remainder	6.6	6.1	6.7	5.1
	Voluntary	6.3	5.2	4.4	4.2
	Forced	5.3	4.8	5.4	4.2

See Table Q (Appendix) for complete data.

continued dissatisfaction with the job itself gradually spreads to other areas.

SUMMARY REMARKS

The recruits who for one reason or another did not stay in the Bell System form a special group within the Management Progress Study. For the most part, however, after all the data are reviewed, it seems that the total group that left are different from the total group that stayed only in the fact that they left. It is true, of course, that the forced terminators differed in many ways from the voluntary terminators, but there are comparable differences among those who did not leave. Some still on the payroll are no more capable than some who were fired, and some of those who left voluntarily are certainly the equal of many who stayed.

There is one striking exception to the generalization that the total group of separatees is not much different from the total group of permanent employees. This is in respect to the top 10 percent of the recruits in management ability. Only one of this group left the Bell System. The terminators included many capable recruits, but very few of the truly outstanding. With this exception, the total group of terminators resembled the stayers in background characteristics, performance at assessment, and even attitudes toward the company. It is this similarity that renders termination hard to predict.

Progress in prediction will clearly come from different directions for voluntary and for forced terminations. We can begin to avoid forced termination by instituting more effective selection standards to assure the requisite ability and motivation to perform. Voluntary termination may prove very difficult to predict at the time of employment, but it can be reduced by attention to the job itself.

12

CAREERS AND PERSONALITY

The findings of the Management Progress Study will, it is hoped, afford useful guidance to organizations in formulating management manpower policies. Some recommendations to this end are presented in Chapter 13. In this chapter we draw some conclusions concerning the relationships between careers in a large organization and the personality patterns of those who experience them. What do the Study results have to say about personality and life orientation over the early adult years?

CHANGES IN THE RECRUITS

One of the clearest personal changes in this group of young recruits was a rapid and decisive move in the direction of greater realism concerning the job. At the outset of the Study most of the subjects were assuming that the organization they were entering was a veritable utopia. All bosses would be inspiring leaders, ability was to be quickly recognized and rewarded, peers would be stimulating, and a vice presidency was doubtless lurking somewhere in the future, ready to pounce when the time was ripe.

This unblushing optimism faded rapidly, and even the first few years of employment saw a decline in the attitudes toward and beliefs about the company. The change did not carry on to a flatly negative or pessimistic outlook, of course. General feelings toward the company retained their positive coloring, even as they fell from the stratosphere of optimism. In a few years the fourth level of management rather than the sixth or seventh typified an ambitious goal for the average man. The ease with which the subjects modified their work perceptions was striking.

One of the heartening findings was the continuation of cognitive development. Not only did the average scores on mental ability tests increase significantly over the eight years, but knowledge of contemporary affairs showed an important advance. In recent years psychologists have devoted much discussion to the question of whether mental ability continues to develop over the adult years. The Study data support the view that the young are not on a downward slide intellectually after they leave college. Incidentally, we can only speculate on the implications of this evidence regarding the so-called generation gap. If young people continue to grow intellectually and to gain in their grasp of world events as they mature following college, how much confidence can we place in the popular charge that an older generation has much to learn about "current" life from a younger generation?

The recruits learned a great deal about the telephone business and the methods of large organizations in general during their early years of employment. There is no doubt that the subjects of the Study became more useful managers over the period of study. There had been a school of thought in the Bell System which held that college recruits were probably intellectually and managerially superior to existing middle managers, even at the time of original employment. The data do not support this view. It seems clear that there is much to be learned as well as much that is learned, in the job experience *per se*. This activity seems to be related to the growing cognitive abilities of the subjects, and in the years to come it will be interesting to see if this growth is sustained.

Turning to the specifics of personality, there was a clear trend in the direction of better adjustment and more independence. Eight years after the start of the Study, the average recruit possessed more motivation for autonomy, less for deference toward authority figures, and less need to affiliate with peers. Concomitantly, there was a noticeable "hardening" in interpersonal motivations. The average recruit rose in his motivations for dominance and aggressiveness. We cannot be certain of the last-named trend for personality development. Is it only a reflection of the growing confidence and self-reliance of men who are in the midst of family and career development? Or is it prompted by the business atmosphere?

It would be helpful if comparative data were available on young men who had entered such clearly nonbusiness professions as social work or the ministry. Would a comparable toughening of personality be found? Lacking such data, only speculation is possible, but the issue is not without a sense of coherence. Taking into account the growing realism and rising grasp of world events manifested by the subjects, this overall personality change would seem to be due more to "growing up" than it is to any peculiarity of the business world.

The young men of the sample displayed a growing *sophistication.* The typical recruit became more worldly wise, if a little disillusioned; in the main he grew distrustful of simplistic solutions, if also at times wary of the spontaneous and shared aspects of social life. In line with his growing technical skills, he emphasized the well-reasoned, the factual, and the realities of what "is possible" to achieve rather than the "pie in the sky" aspirations of his earlier years on the job. Such developments may be peculiar to the business world, but they do not seem to be entirely divorced from what has been said about maturing man for centuries.

These general trends are enriched by a consideration of some differences between the recruits who had reached middle management by the time of reassessment and those who had not. The more successful men became more work oriented, whereas the less successful men became more involved in their families and in their religious, recreational, and social activities.

Indeed, it was fascinating to note how quickly some recruits "gave up" on the work sphere in favor of other life involvements. It had been expected that men who were not especially successful during the early years of their work would redouble their efforts and essentially become *more* job-involved during their first half-dozen years at work. After all, these recruits were still young, their time investment in the company was not lengthy, and a shaky start can be rectified through increased effort in the work sphere. Yet here was what amounted to withdrawal from the job and settling into other life spheres on the part of men who only a few years before had projected rather glowing futures for themselves. What could underlie this phenomenon?

THE IMPORTANCE OF LIFE STYLE

It is not unusual for psychologists to answer such a question on the assumption that the pattern of involvement or withdrawal was *due to* the positive or negative circumstances of the work sphere on the individual. A man who is positively rewarded or "reinforced" from the outset on the job continues to further this activity thanks to the good feelings such recognition, material gain, or power afford him. A man who is comparably negatively reinforced on the job is quickly pushed by this circumstance into a relative withdrawal from the work sphere in his efforts to find positive rewards in life elsewhere.

This line of theoretical speculation has historical precedence second to none in psychology, and it would be easy enough to construe the present data in these terms; nevertheless, the authors have found, after considerable study of the results, that such a framework simply does not capture the life *as lived* by the individual subject. We believe the Study data show quite definitely that the recruits were not passive raw material to be conditioned by the company which employed them into "organization men" of varying levels of success. On the contrary, it appears that given even minimally favorable conditions, careers in the clear majority of cases tended to reflect the kinds of recruits who entered the business. Each man brought with him a developed pattern of abilities and motives which tended to actualize itself in the organizational environment, almost in the sense of a self-fulfilling prophecy.

When we speak of the pattern of behavior that a man brings to an organization, the issue of how life moulds this pattern seems merely to have been pushed back a notch in time. Any pattern isolated can be said to have been a product of even earlier reinforcements, taking the man into one life style or another. The Management Progress Study cannot be expected to enter into this question of the ultimate source of behavioral shaping—whether by the individual, by his environment, or by both combined in some fashion. But as far as the present data are concerned, the man contributes to his eventual job involvement and success in a way that only makes sense if the individual is viewed as an active agent in the course of events.

ENLARGING AND ENFOLDING STYLES

The terminology of Chapter 8, which suggested an enlarging versus an enfolding life style or orientation, conveniently captures the summary impressions that emerge in the total data array. These construct labels were *not* in the collection of theoretical terms brought to bear in the Management Progress Study at its inception. They appeared as identifiable patterns only after the data had been collected and a scoring of the first few companies had been completed. At first the labels were considered primarily in terms of a single company, possibly tied to only certain sociocultural backgrounds; but in time it seemed that they could be used in a global sense. Although the labels are merely abstractions chosen for convenience (other terms might well be substituted), these rubrics are used here for a consideration of career style, personality, and life orientation.

It will be recalled that the Enlarger is one who places emphasis on extension of influence outward into the work and community spheres, seeks expanding responsibilities, and is not strongly attached to past ties. The Enfolder is not greatly concerned with extending himself into new involvements and responsibilities; he values old ties and tends to deepen them rather than breaking with the past. These may be thought of as unnamed premises, used as what the existentialists have called "world designs" to be furthered as future possibilities over life's way. Although secondary attitudes and belief systems are framed by these premises, they need not themselves be articulated verbally (consciously) by the individual holding to them.

It was the Enlarging recruit who usually commanded the better ratings during original assessment; thus an individual evidencing this general life orientation was more likely to be seen as achieving a middle management level early in career development. Moreover, this broad prediction proved to be correct. It was as if the young men had presented themselves to the assessment staff just as they were subsequently to present themselves to their work associates and superiors. They were drawn to the more challenging aspects of a work setting—reaching out to make learning more likely, and thereby extending their scope. Job-related activities such as night school or community involvement seemed to be a natural extension of what the life period (young business man) called for.

The Enfolder, on the other hand, was less preoccupied with the work environment right from the outset. He may have shared the early optimism of the Enlarger; but he did not advance on the work sphere with quite the same thrust of expectation, nor did he demand more of himself and more of his work than the job at that point might have had to offer. Demanding more, the Enlarger made it more likely that he would receive greater job challenge as the months slipped by. This pattern is somewhat analogous to distinctions often drawn between a job and a career, or a worker and a professional. Professions and careers are eked out or made as the individual moves along. Working at jobs is a routine, passive affair of meeting the expectations of others. The Enlarger therefore had much greater professional and career orientation than the Enfolder.

In the analysis of job challenges given the men, an Enlarger was much more likely to be put in a favorable circumstance early in his career development than was an Enfolder. This event was *not* based on an intelligence factor. The work supervisors were not parceling out job assignments according to IQ level. They seemed to be cognizant of the same type of life orientation that the assessment staff had judged so favorably. This individual—the Enlarger—was not to be denied; he came at one with a capacity and an intention to further his life in this work sphere. Indeed, even when the Enlarging individual left the company and took up his career in another industry, the follow-up data suggest that he was more successful in accomplishing career goals (job level, income) than was the Enfolder who left the telephone company. The foregoing observations merely underscore the reasons for feeling that to assign job success and satisfaction to what the company does for the man, rather than also recognizing the reverse direction of influence, is to misconstrue the basic meaning of a life style. It is tempting to speculate on whether it would be possible to convert an Enfolder to an Enlarging life style—or vice versa. What evidence there is from individual life histories indicates that for this to occur, some rather broad-ranged alterations in the total life pattern would be required. In arraying his life style the Enlarger is setting a broad pattern that will sustain his premises about the meaning of life. He presumably meets and marries a woman with the same general outlook, and this relationship provides him support for the commitment to job and community that he eventually furthers.

The Enfolder, on the other hand, arrays a life pattern that focuses more on the nonjob facets of life. He too meets and marries a woman with values comparable to his own life style. Any shift on his part may well upset the balance established, which in turn is confirmation that his unnamed premises are under challenge. To succeed in the work sphere is often to move away from parental and in-law ties and to break up long-standing friendships. Such life developments are by definition undesirable to the Enfolder. Hence it seems unlikely that he is going to place himself in the position of altering his world design unless a broad and deep change occurs, such as a death in the marital or paternal family, a divorce, or an equally dramatic circumstance.

It should be emphasized that questions of personal happiness or judgments of what life style is "best" for a satisfying existence must be left completely aside. The data afford no evidence that an Enlarger finds more fulfillment in his overall life style than does the Enfolder. It is a mistake to reify these two theoretical designations. However, it has occurred to the Study interviewers from time to time that something akin to one pattern is being lived by a man with predilections toward the other. It seems reasonable to assume that a conflict does at times occur—possibly in many people—over which of these value lines to stress.

It is popular today to think of business life as the source of those materialistic values which are being called into daily question. Is not the Enlarger actually a kind of materialistic hustler, who dashes about placing himself in power positions within the "system," while the Enfolder feathers his nest in a more humanistic and sensitively interpersonal way? The authors could not find justification for this parallel. The Enfolders seemed to be no less tied to the system's value structure than the Enlargers. There were as many rebels among Enlarging types, some of whom proved to be highly innovative on the job, as there were among the Enfolders. In fact, a more insightful grasp of what moved the Enlargers tends to negate the argument for materialistic motives. These individuals seemed to be as interested in acquiring ideas, scope, and the chance to innovate (change the system) as they were in acquiring homes, automobiles, and clothing.

Some staff members of the Management Progress Study look for a change in life pattern among the Enlargers as middle life approaches. They suspect that the spiritual side of these men will begin to show itself as the subjects age. Investment in religion will develop because the men will begin to ask the kinds of life versus death questions with which religion commonly deals. It would not be surprising to find at this point that the Enlarger will take on an active role in some church group.

CONFLICTED STYLES

One of the more interesting speculations dealing with the life orientation has to do with what might be termed as a quasi-Enlarger or a quasi-Enfolder. The reference here is to the approximations to the overall pattern of life orientation attained by the false positives and false negatives (see Chapter 8). The recruits who were predicted to reach middle management but did not do so (false positives) had a noticeable component of the Enfolding pattern in that they were much higher on the Recreational-Social and Religious-Humanism themes than were the true positives. On the other hand, among those who were predicted *not* to attain middle management but in fact did do so (false negatives), we find a pronounced emphasis on Financial-Acquisitive involvements.

It has been noted that it would be wrong to reify the Enlarging versus Enfolding patterns as theoretical constructs or to consider them as "pure" types. Yet the quasi-pattern finding implies that even approximations to the modal patterns may reflect distinctive styles of living predictive of job success. No attempt has yet been made to identify individual men with what might be termed "mixed" patterns in life style—as, for example, combining *high* Financial-Acquisitive and Paternal-Familial with *low* Occupational and Religious-Humanism. Such a combination might well herald a conflict-prone existence for the man so involved, at least in that sense just referred to as the clash of values attached to the modal life styles. Settling the issue in one or the other direction should come as a relief for a man in this life circumstance. A study of the patterning of life themes into various clusters on this order remains to be done.

It is also believed that when the life themes are analyzed in terms of such varied clusters, more personality test data may come into the findings. Except for the general group trends already discussed, the results on personality change were limited. Personality has been found to be highly stable in most longitudinal studies to date. Even so, the authors believe that some more intricate patterns of change may have been masked in the analyses done for the present volume, and not until the personality data are rearrayed in terms of life themes will more final answers become known.

Even though the last word has not been expressed, the authors feel confident that the recruits themselves, first seen soon after employment, had a great deal to do with the course of their future lives. They were not developed, trained, and motivated by "Ma Bell" so much as they tended to further the premising implications of an ongoing life style formulated long before they came to the System recruiter. This is not to say that rewards were handed out with perfect equity or that by an improved use of organizational resources a more satisfying arrangement might not have been worked out for all concerned. Nevertheless, these young men must be seen as active shapers of their own careers and life styles.

13

IMPLICATIONS FOR LARGE ORGANIZATIONS

The large organization, whether business or governmental, must continuously advance into its middle ranks numbers of managers who can perform well and who will constitute the pool of senior officers of the future. This book has reported on the early careers of 274 college graduates who were recruited by the Bell System with the expectation that they would help to fill this need. This final chapter examines the implications of the findings for attacking the problem of the supply of middle and upper management. The major finding of the Management Progress Study in this respect is the extreme importance of the accurate selection of the individuals chosen to constitute the management pool.

SOME MISLEADING HOPES

The Study provides no support for the notion that experience is the best teacher or that mediocre recruits will catch fire on the job and turn into world beaters. On the contrary, the average recruit did not improve in his management abilities, even after eight years on the job. This is not to say that a few men did not outperform expectations, but the likelihood of some exceptions to the general finding is not a safe ground for corporate policy.

Another comforting idea espoused by many is that the first year or two of experience will provide a testing ground for management recruits. Those without appreciable potential skill will, it is hoped, become discouraged and resign or will be let go by their supervisors. This belief in the power of attrition to purify the recruit stream is also unsupported by the Study data. Insofar as potential to reach the first rung of middle management is concerned, attrition had no effect on the general quality of the group of subjects. It is true that the less capable recruits were asked to leave a little more often than the more capable, but this tendency was counterbalanced by the greater number of the more capable who left voluntarily. The separation route is not a viable corrective to employment errors.

THE IMPORTANCE OF SELECTION AND PLANNING

The careers of the subjects who showed especially good potential at the time of employment dramatically underline the importance of selection. Here we refer to the 10 percent of the recruits whom the assessment staff found capable of advancing beyond the first middle management step. Of this group of 27 men, only one had left the company, and fifteen had reached middle management by the time of reassessment. Thus approximately 56 percent of the highly assessed group survived and had arrived at middle management in the Bell System, as compared with only 19 percent of all the other recruits originally hired. Although it may be conjectured that attrition even in such a select group would rise if all recruits were of the same calibre, it appears that far fewer recruits would have to be taken on if overall quality were very high.

One additional finding emphasizing the significance of selecting those with the potential to advance is the decline in job motivation and involvement and the development of negative attitudes among those who do not advance. Those with higher potential who do not advance also react negatively, but failure to advance is twice as common among those with lower potential. Hiring recruits who are not likely to advance adds to an organization's motivation and morale problems.

A side of the management employment story that complements the importance of selecting high-quality recruits is the critical need for accurate management manpower planning. Both the quantity and the quality of the management recruits to be sought depend on future requirements. There is no need to charge up a high-powered employment organization or to elevate the expectations of those hired if the number of anticipated openings in middle management is small. If, on the contrary, those openings can be forecast accurately, the whole management employment and advancement system can be made quite efficient. The Study findings indicate that given such accurate predictions and methods of selecting the best recruits, the cost of recruiting and developing future middle management can be greatly reduced. If such recruits were hired and moved expeditiously toward and into middle management, attrition could be expected to be low and loss of motivation minimal. Moreover, the organization could avoid hiring excess numbers of recruits who would fail to reach middle management either because of their own inadequacies or because of the lack of opportunities in the organization.

There are, of course, many management jobs at levels lower than middle management. Although there are no Study data on the point, other evidence would lead to the belief that large organizations can fill such lower management positions from their present employee ranks without special management recruiting. This procedure would have obvious advantages for morale. If this source should prove inadequate and it becomes necessary to make special employment efforts, the Study findings indicate that those who have little chance of reaching middle management should not be led to believe that they are really in the race for such positions.

CONDUCTING EFFECTIVE SELECTION

If selection is so crucial, along what dimensions should recruits for future middle management positions be selected? The Study results reveal six primary clusters of characteristics involved in advancement upward in the management hierarchy.* Although all six are of definite importance, the two most significant factors are leadership skills in face-to-face situations and administrative ability. The four remaining factors, which appear to be of about equal importance, are intellectual ability, stability of performance in the face of stress and uncertainty, and the two clearly motivational factors of work motivation and active career orientation. These dimensions are not completely independent of one another. Administrative skills, for example, are correlated with intellectual ability and leadership skills with stability of performance.

It is the author's conviction that typical college graduate employment procedures do not afford an adequate basis for evaluating potential recruits on the dimensions shown by the Study to be highly related to success. The usual employment procedure involves several interviews and an inspection of the application form. The raw material on which judgments are based is, therefore, of two types—the behavior of the candidate in the interviews, and the candidate's past record as summarized by the candidate either orally or in writing.

Analysis of the Study's assessment data indicates that the interview can provide the material on which to make reliable judgments of important personal characteristics, particularly the dimensions of work motivation and career orientation. It must be emphasized, however, that the value of material thus obtained was demonstrated by trained raters reading the interview reports and applying common standards to them all. In addition, the interviewers in the Study were well-trained professionals who spent at least an hour and a half with the interviewee before dictating lengthy reports. These conditions are seldom—one is tempted to say never—present in ordinary college recruiting. Nevertheless, the interview is a very good potential basis for judgments of motivation important to success in management.

The evaluation of a third factor, intellectual ability, can be readily accomplished simply by administering a standardized

---

* An additional factor, dependence on others, listed in Chapter 7, was of statistical significance but of less importance than those discussed here.

paper-and-pencil test. Only a minority of business organizations, however, actually include this technique in their college employment procedures. When no test is given, inferences about mental ability are sometimes made from grade-point average, rank in graduating class, and quality of college attended. Although these indirect clues are, of course, correlated with measured mental ability, they are by no means an adequate substitute for testing.

Some organizations are not interested in a refined measure of mental ability because it is believed that graduation from even the average college is evidence of sufficient intelligence for a management career. Given that minimum, it is sometimes believed, "other factors take over" and determine success. This notion is incorrect. Although a high degree of mental ability unaccompanied by certain other characteristics is of little value in a management career, those other characteristics are much less likely to lead to success when mental ability is below the managerial average.

Thus without any radical change in the procedures employed, organizations have the means to evaluate three of the factors that were shown by the Study to be important determinants of progress in management—work motivation, career orientation, and intellectual ability. In the case of the other three dimensions—administrative skills, leadership, and stability of performance—more ambitious methods are required. It appears probable that most college employment people do not even attempt to judge administrative skills or stability of performance. They do often make judgments of leadership ability on the basis of information about extracurricular activities during school and college years. There is some validity to this process, although the tendency to confuse football playing with leadership is difficult to suppress.

Even at best, however, such indirect evidence is a weak substitute for direct observation of administrative and interpersonal behavior. In the assessment center, the In-Basket afforded the opportunity to observe administrative skills, planning and organizing, and decision making under standardized conditions. The leaderless group discussion and the business game provided the basis for the evaluation of leadership and stability of performance. The success of the assessment center in predicting progress, and the importance of such simulation techniques in the assessment process, lead clearly to the conclusion that assessment of management recruits would greatly increase accuracy in the employment process.

Complete assessment cannot be accomplished in less than two very full days of a candidate's time, and a group of five or six candidates must be available simultaneously. Some managements may be reluctant to use the method because of the problems created by such constraints, but they are by no means insoluble. We have learned that most potential management recruits are not only willing to spend the time to be assessed but find it is a valuable experience. Because of the cost of assessment operations, however, screening of applicants prior to assessment is in order.

Where preemployment assessment is not undertaken, there is still a valuable possible application of the method during the early months of a recruit's employment. Assessment results can be considered along with job performance in diagnosing development needs, as well as in deciding which recruits show good promise and which should be asked to leave. Since those to be assessed are on the payroll, it is easy to schedule assessment groups.

THE IMPORTANCE OF THE JOB

The use of advanced selection methods can enable an organization to provide itself with a pool of high-potential recruits to be the middle and upper managers of the future. These resources can easily be wasted, however, unless the organization takes steps to furnish job experiences that sustain the motivation high-quality recruits bring with them. The Study data show declines, often quite sharp, in expectations and attitudes soon after employment. These changes are partly the result of reality impinging on impossibly high initial hopes. They are also attributable to a failure for promotions to develop. Better management manpower planning can forestall some of these disappointments.

Over and above these factors, however, the Study points to the need for stimulation and challenge in the work itself. As we certainly would expect, the importance of work in one's life scheme appears to depend on how rewarding the work is. Many of the recruits reacted to lack of job challenge rather quickly. The Study period reported in this volume, after all, covered only eight years of careers that may run as long as 35 to 40 years. Management must attempt to provide early and rapidly expanding challenges if motivation is to be maintained at a high level.

Perhaps at least some of those who have become demotivated might be brought back to more positive motivation by being assigned to a highly challenging situation. Such a result is not unknown. It is not, however, likely to occur in the normal course of things. The Study suggests, on the contrary, a circular process in which the more highly motivated individuals receive the more challenging assignments which, in turn, sustain their high motivation. Those who are less motivated tend to receive the more routine assignments.

Organizations run two risks—they may fail to recruit and employ those with high managment potential, or they may lose much of the contribution that high-potential people can make by reducing their job involvement. Organizations must avoid *both* these dangers or management development efforts will always be at least partial failures. There is no lack of knowledge about how organizations can be highly successful in these regards, yet it appears that the inertia and resistances that preclude improvement are seldom overcome.

APPENDIX

The tables that follow present the complete data from which many of the tables and all the figures in the text were derived. The data are reproduced for the benefit of those who wish to study them in detail.

The reader will note that the numbers of cases (Ns) vary considerably from table to table and frequently within tables. A major factor in the variability of Ns arises from the inclusion of the Michigan Bell sample in some instances and its omission in others. In Table G, for example, the Michigan sample was not administered the School and College Ability Test (SCAT) at assessment but was administered the test at reassessment. This means, of course, that the correlation coefficients shown and the t tests for the SCAT comparisons were based on the common N (i.e., 123), rather than on the N of 167, as they were for the Critical Thinking and Contemporary Affairs tests.

Another source of variability in the Ns is that of missing data. For example, not all of the assessment and reassessment interviews (Table K) could be coded on each variable. Nor were all the participants in the Study available for each follow-up interview (Table B).

The reader may also note that the correlation coefficients between assessment and reassessment ratings or scores (Tables E-K) are not commented on in the text. These coefficients are of interest and did, of course, enter into computation of the t tests. The coefficients vary considerably, indicating that some characteristics, or measures thereof, are more stable over time than others. The absence of comment in the text was occasioned by a primary concern for reporting on group comparisons rather than on individual change.

Finally, we note that the statistical tests reported are those discussed in the text and those which influenced interpretations of the data. Thus in Tables L through O, the F ratios given are those for interactions between groups and trials (assessment-reassessment).

A study of this magnitude generates a very large volume of data. The authors have been selective both in making analyses and in reporting the salient results. It is expected that many more analyses will be made and that articles will be published on the findings.

APPENDIX TABLES

Table A. Correlations of Assessment Methods with Scores Based on Assessment Factors[1]

Method	Administrative Skills	Interpersonal Skills	Intellectual Ability	Stability of Performance	Work Motivation	Career Orientation[2]	Dependency
In-Basket	76**	45**	36**	39**	44**	18**	−15*
Manufacturing Problem							
Observer rating	31**	39**	18**	37**	30**	35**	−18**
Peer rating	24**	29**	11	22**	28**	28**	−15*
Self rating	03	11	04	13	10	26**	−17*
Group Discussion							
Observer rating (overall)	48**	62**	27**	47**	45**	39**	−22**
Observer rating (oral presentation)	42**	52**	26**	32**	34**	29**	−07
Peer rating	41**	52**	31**	36**	40**	37**	−20**
Self rating	19**	23**	10	21**	18**	28**	−14*

School and College Ability Test						
Verbal	37**	22**	79**	23**	17*	16*	−17*
Quantitative	16*	−03	29**	09	05	00	−20**
Total	34**	13	70**	21**	14*	10	−24**
Contemporary Affairs Test	30**	19**	73**	20**	14*	10	−14*
Critical Thinking in Social Science Test	34**	20**	65**	16*	14*	16*	−19**
Interview rating on						
Forcefulness	42**	44**	22**	29**	36**	38**	−16*
Oral Communication Skills	33**	36**	40**	23**	26**	26**	−06
Human Relations Skills	16*	28**	06	23**	19*	25**	−14
Likeableness	22*	39**	04	13	31**	03	−01
Behavior Flexibility	12	21**	09	18**	10	16*	−12
Need for Superior Approval	−11	−05	−08	−14	03	−20*	27**
Need for Peer Approval	−22**	−12	−16*	−16*	−08	−24**	25**
Tolerance of Uncertainty	17*	20**	18**	30**	15*	26**	−20**
Inner Work Standards	10	18**	09	19**	40**	16*	−03
Primacy of Work	13	16*	05	19*	35**	22**	−10
Energy	20**	30**	05	26**	24**	32**	−15*

Table A. Correlations of Assessment Methods with Scores Based on Assessment Factors[1]

Method	Assessment Factor						
	Administrative Skills	Interpersonal Skills	Intellectual Ability	Stability of Performance	Work Motivation	Career Orientation[2]	Dependency
Goal Flexibility	-20**	-20**	-13	-19**	-31**	-24**	13
Need Advancement	27**	23**	23**	23**	27**	57**	-24**
Need Security	-17*	-23**	-29**	-23**	-19*	-50**	21**
Social Objectivity	10	10	19*	13	17*	00	-01
Bell System Value Orientation	-06	-03	-17*	-06	01	-12	05
Ability to Delay Gratification	00	-06	02	04	-03	-10	-01
Range of Interests	14*	24**	35**	13	15*	05	11
Projective ratings on							
Optimism–Pessimism	08	17*	-05	19**	16*	10	-06
General Adjustment	23**	21**	-01	28**	23**	18**	-19**
Self-Confidence	21**	17*	04	24**	15*	39**	-33**
Affiliation	-08	07	-08	-01	13	-26**	46**
Work or Career Orientation	29**	17*	10	13	50**	14*	03

Leadership Role	36**	20**	22**	29**	25**	47**	−49**
Dependence	−30**	−16*	−33***	−28***	−05	−39***	49***
Subordinate Role	−24***	−05	−27***	−12	02	−36***	38***
Achievement Motivation	33**	12	20***	12	33**	41**	−24***
Scores on Rotter Incomplete Sentences Blank	−09	−03	05	−13	11	−09	22**
Scores on Edwards Personal Preference Schedule—Need for							
Achievement	06	06	12	10	21**	15*	−29**
Deference	−03	04	−01	01	22**	−04	12
Order	−07	−08	−04	−03	05	−11	05
Exhibition	08	07	08	06	05	16*	−12
Autonomy	−02	−12	05	05	−07	00	−12
Affiliation	05	14*	05	−11	05	−03	13
Intraception	05	−05	05	08	−01	02	−04
Succorance	−09	−01	−18**	−23**	−01	−17*	24**
Dominance	30**	27**	07	26**	28**	27**	−22**
Abasement	−12	−07	−23**	−09	−13	−20**	21**
Nurturance	−03	10	−08	−09	−00	−04	21**
Change	−13	−08	03	−01	−18**	04	−11
Endurance	−03	−03	−02	02	07	−10	11
Heterosexuality	−02	−03	08	−03	−13	−01	−04
Aggression	03	−01	03	06	−06	10	−20**

Table A. Correlations of Assessment Methods with Scores Based on Assessment Factors[1]

	Assessment Factor						
Method	Administrative Skills	Interpersonal Skills	Intellectual Ability	Stability of Performance	Work Motivation	Career Orientation[2]	Dependency
Scores on Guilford-Martin Inventory of Factors GAMIN							
General Activity	16*	16*	02	19**	11	43**	−23**
Ascendancy	19**	18**	−05	28**	15*	35**	−23**
Masculinity	10	−10	−03	01	06	08	−13
Self-Confidence	09	03	−09	12	07	14*	−20**
Lack of Nervousness	12	02	−04	06	15*	06	−09

* Significant at .05 level (N = 207 for all but interview ratings, which vary from 111 to 198).
** Significant at .01 level (N = 207 for all but interview ratings).

[1] Decimal point omitted.
[2] High scores on Career Orientation reflect high ratings on Need Advancement and low ratings on Need Security and Ability to Delay Gratification.

Table B. Life Themes—Means and Standard Deviations for the Total Group, by Year

			Time Interviewed														
	Assessment (N = 167)		Year 1 (N = 132)		Year 2 (N = 137)		Year 3 (N = 156)		Year 4 (N = 162)		Year 5 (N = 161)		Year 6 (N = 157)		Year 7 (N = 166)	
Theme	Mean	S.D.	Mean	S.D.	Mean	S.D.	Mean	S.D.	Mean	S.D.	Mean	S.D.	Mean	S.D.	Mean	S.D.
Current Occupational	15.73	2.88	16.33	3.85	16.83	4.29	16.96	5.75	16.87	4.97	18.08	4.96	17.45	5.54	17.31	5.70
Ego Functional	16.73	2.34	16.24	3.50	15.97	3.78	15.54	3.41	15.44	3.77	15.79	4.06	15.84	4.73	15.62	4.06
Financial-Acquisitive	16.60	2.52	16.84	2.51	17.21	2.95	17.37	3.11	17.81	3.35	18.05	3.61	18.89	3.88	18.64	3.86
Locale-Residential	17.14	2.90	16.91	2.47	16.96	2.62	17.10	2.97	17.09	3.34	17.29	3.10	18.38	3.58	17.15	3.07
Marital-Familial	16.95	3.23	18.03	3.35	18.18	4.09	18.14	4.10	18.50	4.29	19.10	4.28	19.42	4.42	19.71	4.28
Parental-Familial	18.26	3.31	17.40	3.75	17.15	4.04	16.64	4.41	16.28	4.28	16.34	4.50	16.20	4.59	15.90	4.62
Recreational-Social	16.55	2.82	16.33	3.38	15.66	3.70	15.65	4.20	15.48	4.07	15.80	4.04	15.60	4.41	15.43	4.58
Religious-Humanism	16.82	3.53	16.64	4.14	15.63	4.60	15.75	5.19	15.90	5.10	15.99	5.05	16.15	5.95	16.35	5.66
Service	16.20	2.56	15.02	3.59	14.35	3.80	14.55	4.19	14.67	4.78	14.93	5.02	14.84	4.65	14.53	4.77

Table C. Life Themes—Comparisons of those Who Did and Did Not Reach Middle Management

	Means and Standard Deviations by Follow-up Date							
	Assessment		Year 1		Year 2		Year 3	
Theme and Group[1]	Mean	S.D.	Mean	S.D.	Mean	S.D.	Mean	S.D.
Current Occupational								
Achieved middle management	16.76	2.85	17.49	3.72	18.39	3.85	18.45	4.61
Did not achieve middle management	15.11	2.59	14.84	3.52	14.67	3.94	14.28	4.21
Ego Functional								
Achieved middle management	17.42	2.18	16.94	3.30	16.77	3.34	15.99	3.23
Did not achieve middle management	15.87	2.04	14.97	3.00	14.75	3.62	14.40	3.21
Marital-Familial								
Achieved middle management	17.02	3.24	17.28	3.42	17.53	4.02	17.64	3.95
Did not achieve middle management	16.30	3.18	17.79	3.14	17.61	4.02	17.80	4.07
Financial-Acquisitive								
Achieved middle management	16.99	2.41	16.75	2.23	17.30	2.94	17.43	2.88
Did not achieve middle management	15.98	2.95	16.59	2.79	16.74	3.05	16.96	3.22
Parental-Familial								
Achieved middle management	18.17	2.94	17.13	3.35	16.69	4.13	15.83	4.63
Did not achieve middle management	17.87	3.49	17.68	4.03	17.64	3.98	17.50	4.56
Recreational-Social								
Achieved middle management	16.15	2.41	15.75	2.87	15.35	3.47	14.81	3.86
Did not achieve middle management	16.75	3.04	16.49	3.32	15.79	3.54	15.54	4.31
Locale-Residential								
Achieved middle management	17.20	2.72	17.11	2.36	17.29	2.82	17.27	2.84
Did not achieve middle management	16.77	3.02	16.81	2.84	16.84	2.64	17.02	2.91
Religious-Humanism								
Achieved middle management	16.22	3.68	16.30	4.05	15.44	4.62	15.12	4.88
Did not achieve middle management	17.24	3.00	17.04	3.82	16.20	4.11	16.42	5.05
Service								
Achieved middle management	16.05	2.40	15.04	3.42	14.99	3.76	15.50	4.06
Did not achieve middle management	15.90	2.63	14.82	3.60	14.28	3.75	13.35	3.90

[1] Number of cases in each group = 61.

Means and Standard Deviations by Follow-up Date								Analysis of Variance		
Year 4		Year 5		Year 6		Year 7				Sig-
Mean	S.D.	Mean	S.D.	Mean	S.D.	Mean	S.D.	Source	F Ratio	nificance Level
18.89	4.48	20.07	4.80	20.39	4.94	21.05	5.00	Groups	63.43	<.01
								Years	4.54	<.01
14.60	5.17	15.58	4.54	13.66	4.06	12.99	3.97	Interaction	13.67	<.01
15.57	3.66	17.02	4.96	16.47	4.04	16.69	4.02	Groups	15.17	<.01
								Years	6.06	<.01
14.38	3.68	14.25	3.80	14.11	3.48	14.21	4.03	Interaction	1.89	>.05
17.84	4.24	18.42	3.83	18.58	3.99	18.99	4.38	Groups	2.01	>.05
								Years	18.88	<.01
18.27	3.96	19.07	4.05	19.70	3.98	20.08	4.13	Interaction	1.85	>.05
17.63	2.94	18.10	2.96	18.84	3.43	19.02	3.23	Groups	0.83	>.05
								Years	14.96	<.01
17.56	3.54	17.61	3.90	17.84	3.85	17.61	4.15	Interaction	0.16	>.05
15.44	4.57	15.10	4.93	15.59	4.83	14.05	4.64	Groups	4.04	<.05
								Years	12.05	<.01
16.96	4.48	17.15	4.52	16.62	4.72	17.07	4.54	Interaction	4.52	<.01
14.69	3.77	14.91	4.01	14.33	4.15	14.47	4.60	Groups	1.04	>.05
								Years	7.50	<.01
15.44	4.19	15.98	4.13	15.65	4.37	15.39	4.63	Interaction	1.01	>.05
17.37	3.45	17.82	2.85	17.33	3.18	17.80	3.38	Groups	1.32	>.05
								Years	1.24	>.05
16.96	3.48	17.14	3.36	16.77	3.07	16.84	3.30	Interaction	0.66	>.05
14.99	4.87	15.20	4.76	14.92	4.31	14.88	5.14	Groups	4.00	<.05
								Years	3.20	<.01
16.42	5.06	16.62	5.12	16.88	5.10	17.93	6.08	Interaction	2.60	<.01
15.80	4.67	15.91	4.98	15.45	4.55	15.50	4.73	Groups	5.74	<.01
								Years	4.44	<.01
13.53	4.71	14.17	5.15	13.62	4.57	13.04	4.97	Interaction	3.43	<.01

Table D. Life Themes—Comparisons of Prediction Groups (True Positives, False Positives, False Negatives, True Negatives)

Theme and Group[1]	Assessment		Date Interviewed													
			Year 1		Year 2		Year 3		Year 4		Year 5		Year 6		Year 7	
	Mean	S.D.	Mean	S.D.	Mean	S.D.	Mean	S.D.	Mean	S.D.	Mean	S.D.	Mean	S.D.	Mean	S.D.
Current Occupational																
True positive	17.71	2.88	18.87	3.71	19.62	3.75	19.76	4.38	20.13	4.54	21.50	4.83	21.64	4.67	22.21	4.89
False positive	14.80	2.09	15.47	3.70	16.50	4.56	18.88	10.45	16.47	4.37	17.55	3.67	15.53	4.32	14.05	5.09
False negative	15.10	2.00	14.24	1.93	15.72	3.10	15.97	4.19	16.58	3.77	17.38	4.12	18.21	5.49	18.95	4.94
True negative	14.21	2.31	14.40	3.74	14.03	3.89	13.95	4.57	13.81	5.17	15.64	4.58	14.53	4.59	13.55	4.17
Ego Functional																
True positive	17.81	2.21	17.67	3.40	17.49	3.36	16.86	2.87	16.42	3.51	17.16	3.35	16.77	3.21	17.46	3.84
False positive	16.18	1.72	16.28	3.02	16.83	4.50	15.50	3.67	15.55	3.35	15.64	3.48	17.15	8.32	16.27	3.51
False negative	16.83	2.11	14.82	2.57	14.63	2.67	13.66	2.86	13.70	3.50	15.43	5.02	14.89	5.11	14.85	3.95
True negative	15.94	1.98	14.81	4.12	14.15	3.42	14.76	3.73	14.03	4.01	14.09	4.52	14.10	4.42	13.72	4.48
Financial-Acquisitive																
True positive	17.49	2.12	17.21	2.21	17.55	2.70	17.88	2.33	17.77	2.32	18.29	2.18	18.93	2.80	19.53	2.72
False positive	16.25	2.80	17.25	2.76	16.94	3.30	17.00	3.40	17.24	2.08	17.12	2.66	17.39	2.14	17.68	3.44
False negative	16.30	2.77	15.85	2.32	16.58	3.75	16.47	3.80	17.40	3.98	17.43	4.15	18.58	4.51	18.28	4.12
True negative	15.24	2.29	15.69	2.44	16.34	2.91	15.91	2.59	16.58	3.46	16.79	3.91	17.45	3.72	16.79	3.87
Locale-Residential																
True positive	16.81	2.11	16.71	2.12	17.16	2.87	16.76	2.66	17.04	3.56	17.34	3.00	16.62	2.71	17.27	3.28
False positive	17.09	3.20	16.94	2.58	17.19	2.29	16.98	3.00	16.10	3.19	16.45	2.72	17.20	5.82	16.36	2.70
False negative	17.83	3.60	17.74	2.78	17.56	3.04	18.16	3.23	18.05	3.34	18.53	2.53	18.34	3.82	18.93	3.61
True negative	17.39	3.24	16.58	2.71	16.69	2.30	17.61	3.24	17.56	3.53	17.58	3.76	17.17	3.50	16.84	3.71

Marital-Familial																
True positive	16.97	2.91	17.55	3.37	17.04	3.62	17.19	3.61	17.54	4.48	17.72	4.22	18.05	5.02	18.51	4.66
False positive	16.57	2.46	17.75	3.41	18.17	4.62	17.78	5.58	18.03	3.99	18.17	3.49	19.25	3.70	19.34	3.68
False negative	17.18	3.96	18.15	2.41	19.42	4.53	19.00	4.44	19.03	3.02	20.00	2.81	19.05	3.60	19.83	3.77
True negative	16.54	3.02	18.19	3.61	17.44	4.53	18.22	3.61	18.69	4.23	19.76	4.43	19.92	4.16	20.44	4.34
Parental-Familial																
True positive	17.86	2.97	16.91	3.49	16.05	4.32	14.99	4.76	14.37	4.33	13.95	4.55	14.34	4.78	13.21	4.99
False positive	17.16	3.71	16.14	4.74	15.83	4.85	15.60	4.41	15.66	4.16	16.50	4.69	15.58	5.13	16.45	4.84
False negative	18.60	3.03	16.94	2.66	17.86	3.73	16.89	4.00	16.98	4.35	17.00	5.19	16.79	4.42	15.48	3.83
True negative	18.27	3.24	18.29	3.61	18.02	3.80	17.42	4.80	17.20	4.60	17.78	4.49	17.65	4.76	17.29	4.54
Recreational-Social																
True positive	16.24	2.34	15.59	3.10	15.18	3.58	14.45	3.72	14.32	3.82	14.78	4.31	14.20	4.54	14.15	4.74
False positive	17.02	3.18	17.64	3.54	16.28	4.11	16.65	5.02	16.34	4.56	16.50	3.75	16.26	4.06	15.36	4.14
False negative	15.70	2.42	15.44	2.30	15.19	3.53	14.87	3.93	14.88	3.56	14.75	3.42	13.95	3.46	14.28	3.94
True negative	16.80	2.82	16.16	3.45	15.47	3.69	15.35	4.20	15.28	4.05	16.24	3.89	15.94	4.28	15.74	4.29
Religious-Humanism																
True positive	16.06	3.58	15.82	4.20	14.99	4.63	14.59	4.53	14.85	4.58	14.62	4.50	15.97	5.32	14.31	5.13
False positive	17.73	3.30	18.92	4.19	17.72	4.54	18.23	5.48	18.84	5.32	19.12	5.09	18.18	5.98	18.84	5.93
False negative	16.40	4.18	17.65	3.86	16.22	5.13	16.32	5.58	15.45	5.47	16.73	5.31	15.53	4.77	16.45	5.16
True negative	16.60	3.45	15.71	3.43	15.13	3.97	15.85	4.88	15.96	4.73	16.27	4.81	16.63	4.15	18.29	5.21
Service																
True positive	16.18	2.34	15.22	3.56	15.33	4.04	16.04	4.39	16.47	4.89	16.32	5.43	15.61	5.05	16.17	4.90
False positive	17.25	2.84	16.36	3.03	15.81	3.15	15.90	3.04	15.58	4.78	16.50	5.13	16.16	3.83	15.02	3.05
False negative	15.60	2.62	14.32	3.46	13.93	3.36	14.53	3.49	14.90	4.08	14.78	4.39	14.84	4.13	14.33	4.60
True negative	16.12	2.85	13.98	4.25	13.21	3.86	13.36	4.48	13.80	5.13	14.76	4.99	14.18	5.01	13.60	5.67

[1] Number of cases: true positives = 39; false positives = 22; false negatives = 20; true negatives = 42.

Table E. Changes in Assessment Staff Ratings, Total Group

Variable	Number of Cases Assess-ment	Reassess-ment	Mean Assess-ment	Reassess-ment	Standard Deviation Assess-ment	Reassess-ment	Mean Difference (R − A)	Corre-lation Coefficient	t	Significance Level
Organizing and Planning	124	167	29.35	28.89	8.81	9.72	−0.46	.22	0.61	>.05
Decision Making	124	167	27.74	25.54	8.73	10.40	−2.20	.31	1.76	>.05
Creativity	165	167	25.45	23.41	9.40	9.46	−2.04	.23	2.20	<.05
Oral Communications Skills	167	167	31.02	28.68	9.48	10.30	−2.34	.37	2.71	<.01
Written Communications Skills	69	167	30.72	29.37	8.63	8.73	−1.35	.26	0.51	>.05
Human Relations Skills	167	167	27.37	24.49	8.66	9.67	−2.88	.26	3.33	<.01
Personal Impact— Forcefulness	164	167	27.87	26.62	8.78	9.73	−1.25	.28	1.58	>.05
Personal Impact— Likeableness	69	166	30.14	27.17	8.66	7.62	−2.97	.28	2.52	<.05
Behavior Flexibility	167	167	30.54	25.12	9.77	9.66	−5.42	.22	5.76	<.01

Perception of Threshold									
Social Cues	166	167	30.00	28.50	8.88	8.51	−1.50	.25	1.90	>.05
Scholastic Aptitude	167	167	30.96	33.56	9.95	11.76	2.60	.71	4.00	<.01
Range of Interests	167	167	27.54	27.87	10.32	10.87	0.33	.51	0.40	>.05
Inner Work Standards	164	167	31.52	31.53	9.11	8.98	0.01	.27	0.07	>.05
Primacy of Work	165	167	30.79	31.26	9.04	11.32	0.47	.16	0.41	>.05
Need Advancement	167	167	32.34	31.77	9.44	11.73	−0.57	.26	0.57	>.05
Need Security	165	167	36.12	36.26	8.94	9.01	0.14	.24	0.28	>.05
Ability to Delay Gratification	161	167	33.54	31.74	9.18	10.16	−1.80	.22	1.83	>.05
Resistance to Stress	162	167	29.75	28.50	9.25	9.51	−1.25	.17	1.17	>.05
Tolerance of Uncertainty	163	167	28.16	25.27	9.11	10.11	−2.89	.14	3.04	<.01
Need Approval of									
Superiors	166	167	37.23	32.69	8.14	10.83	−4.54	.34	5.14	<.01
Need Approval of Peers	167	167	33.11	27.40	9.63	10.86	−5.71	.38	6.47	<.01
Goal Flexibility	163	167	31.84	25.39	11.98	9.10	−6.45	.06	5.64	<.01
Energy	166	167	32.23	31.44	8.63	9.82	−0.79	.51	1.02	>.05
Self-Objectivity	166	167	29.94	28.68	8.84	10.31	−1.26	.15	1.24	>.05
Social Objectivity	165	167	27.94	27.90	9.27	11.20	−0.04	.43	0.07	>.05
Bell System Value									
Orientation	165	167	33.27	33.05	10.77	9.69	−0.22	.23	0.09	>.05
Realism of Expectations	165	167	32.73	30.62	9.65	11.32	−2.11	.28	2.02	<.05

Table F. Changes in Assessment Factors, Total Group

Factor	Number of Cases — Assessment and Re-assessment	Mean — Assessment	Mean — Reassessment	Standard Deviation — Assessment	Standard Deviation — Reassessment	Mean Difference (R – A)	Correlation Coefficient	t	Significance Level
Administrative Skills	164	5.69	5.49	1.68	1.94	−0.20	.27	1.16	>.05
Interpersonal skills	164	8.57	7.94	2.22	2.81	−0.63	.27	2.62	<.01
Intellectual abilities	164	5.84	6.15	1.80	1.99	0.31	.68	2.57	<.01
Work motivation	164	6.54	6.51	3.73	2.90	−0.03	.12	0.09	>.05
Career orientation	164	3.91	4.02	3.26	5.73	0.11	.47	0.29	>.05
Stability of performance	164	5.80	5.40	1.57	1.78	−0.40	.20	2.42	<.05
Dependency	164	10.19	8.52	2.37	2.18	−1.67	.31	7.96	<.01

Table G. Changes in Ability Test Scores, Total Group

Test	Number of Cases Assess-ment	Number of Cases Reassess-ment	Mean Assess-ment	Mean Reassess-ment	Standard Deviation Assess-ment	Standard Deviation Reassess-ment	Mean Difference (R − A)	Corre-lation Coefficient	t	Significance Level
School and College Ability										
Verbal	123	167	45.05	49.16	7.09	6.97	4.11	.78	9.93	<.01
Quantitative	123	167	40.98	42.31	7.15	6.77	1.33	.75	3.00	<.01
Total	123	167	86.07	91.93	11.06	11.29	5.86	.77	8.70	<.01
Critical Thinking	167	167	36.45	40.37	6.12	5.43	3.92	.71	11.28	<.01
Contemporary Affairs	167	167	30.76	45.57	25.00	29.14	14.81	.65	8.27	<.01

Table H. Changes in Ratings on Assessment Exercises, Total Group

Exercise	Number of Cases Assess-ment	Number of Cases Reassess-ment	Mean Assess-ment	Mean Reassess-ment	Standard Deviation Assess-ment	Standard Deviation Reassess-ment	Mean Difference (R − A)	Corre-lation Coefficient	t	Significance Level
In-Basket	123	167	2.65	2.89	1.05	1.29	.24	.06	1.51	>.05
Business Games— Observers	123	123	33.54	27.76	8.96	9.04	−5.78	.33	6.14	<.01
Group Discussion										
Observers—oral	123	123	33.70	27.93	8.73	9.45	−5.77	.20	5.67	<.01
Observers—overall	123	123	33.13	26.06	11.19	9.98	−7.07	.31	6.31	<.01

Table I. Changes in Personality Questionnaire Scores, Total Group

Questionnaire	Number of Cases (Assessment and Reassessment)	Mean Assessment	Mean Reassessment	Standard Deviation Assessment	Standard Deviation Reassessment	Mean Difference (R − A)	Correlation Coefficient	t	Significance Level
Edwards Personal Preference Schedule need for									
Achievement	167	17.66	19.90	3.97	3.63	2.24	.40	6.94	<.01
Deference	167	11.92	11.16	3.39	3.22	−0.76	.39	2.69	<.01
Order	167	11.87	11.80	4.52	4.49	−0.07	.59	0.23	>.05
Exhibition	167	15.53	15.17	3.64	3.84	−0.36	.50	1.24	>.05
Autonomy	167	11.79	13.92	4.00	4.22	2.13	.32	5.73	<.01
Affiliation	167	14.74	12.47	3.80	4.05	−2.27	.40	6.84	<.01
Intraception	167	15.59	14.99	4.68	4.82	−0.60	.58	1.78	>.05

	N								
Succorance	167	8.82	8.18	4.70	4.45	−0.64	.49	1.78	>.05
Dominance	167	20.64	21.39	4.02	4.01	0.75	.58	2.64	<.01
Abasement	167	10.56	9.83	4.51	4.50	−0.73	.53	2.16	<.05
Nurturance	167	11.59	11.05	4.36	4.89	−0.54	.53	1.56	>.05
Change	167	16.04	16.38	3.96	4.09	0.34	.37	0.98	>.05
Endurance	167	14.50	14.28	4.78	4.94	−0.22	.51	0.59	>.05
Heterosexuality	167	16.56	16.51	5.69	6.05	−0.05	.43	0.10	>.05
Aggression	167	12.19	12.91	3.90	4.42	0.72	.36	1.98	<.05
Guilford-Martin Inventory of Factors (GAMIN)									
General Activity	167	13.81	14.11	4.54	4.62	0.30	.59	0.93	>.05
Ascendancy	167	26.16	25.25	6.05	6.46	−0.91	.63	2.17	<.05
Masculinity–Femininity	167	25.02	25.57	4.96	4.30	0.55	.51	1.51	>.05
Self-Confidence	167	40.08	38.97	6.85	6.95	−1.11	.48	2.05	<.05
Lack of Nervousness	167	29.07	29.05	6.87	7.16	−0.02	.54	0.00	>.05

Table J. Changes in Projective Variables, Total Group

Variable	Number of Cases (Assessment and Re-assessment)	Mean (Assessment)	Mean (Reassessment)	Standard Deviation (Assessment)	Standard Deviation (Reassessment)	Mean Difference $(R - A)$	Correlation Coefficient	t	Significance Level
Rating on									
Achievement Motivation	167	6.33	6.10	1.95	2.38	−0.23	.19	1.09	>.05
Self-Confidence	167	5.68	6.17	1.69	1.77	0.49	.17	2.85	<.01
Work Orientation	167	6.19	6.14	1.85	2.31	−0.05	.15	0.23	>.05
Dependence	167	6.11	6.14	1.95	2.06	0.03	.30	0.16	>.05
Affiliation	167	6.31	5.87	2.25	2.35	−0.44	.34	2.14	<.05
Optimism–Pessimism	167	6.27	6.46	1.69	1.69	0.19	.14	1.12	>.05
Leadership Role	167	6.01	6.11	1.94	2.03	0.10	.31	0.56	>.05
Subordinate Role	167	6.10	5.78	1.83	1.92	−0.32	.21	1.74	>.05
General Adjustment	167	5.84	6.28	1.48	1.57	0.44	.20	2.92	<.01
Score on Rotter Incomplete Sentences Blank	167	121.02	123.43	12.45	15.81	2.41	.41	1.99	<.05

Table K. Changes in Interview Ratings, Total Group

Variable	Number of Cases Assessment and Reassessment	Mean Assessment	Mean Reassessment	Standard Deviation Assessment	Standard Deviation Reassessment	Mean Difference (R − A)	Correlation Coefficient	t	Significance Level
Oral Communications Skills	100	6.48	6.92	2.12	2.16	0.44	.32	1.69	>.05
Human Relations Skills	82	6.50	6.72	1.70	2.02	0.22	.10	0.76	>.05
Personal Impact—Forcefulness	107	6.11	5.77	2.18	2.46	−0.34	.27	1.27	>.05
Personal Impact—Likeableness	85	7.76	6.68	1.66	2.26	−1.08	.22	3.95	<.01
Social Objectivity	124	5.98	6.96	2.11	2.17	0.98	.15	4.03	<.01
Behavior Flexibility	129	6.58	7.10	1.71	1.79	0.52	.12	2.53	<.05
Need Approval of Superiors	112	7.86	5.77	1.70	2.44	−2.09	.30	8.74	<.01
Need Approval of Peers	41	7.10	6.34	1.75	2.47	−0.76	.08	1.68	>.05
Inner Work Standards	128	7.33	7.90	1.65	1.76	0.57	.21	2.97	<.01
Need Advancement	149	7.02	6.35	1.83	2.12	−0.67	.36	3.59	<.01
Need Security	91	7.15	7.16	2.09	2.28	0.01	.17	0.04	>.05
Goal Flexibility	139	5.33	4.73	1.85	1.96	−0.60	.06	2.73	<.01
Primacy of Work	135	6.50	6.50	1.65	2.27	0.00	.15	0.00	>.05
Bell System Value Orientation	138	7.46	6.93	1.66	2.15	−0.53	−.03	2.28	<.05
Tolerance of Uncertainty	84	5.71	6.48	1.82	1.99	0.77	.06	2.72	<.01
Ability to Delay Gratification	127	5.81	5.92	1.95	2.03	0.11	−.18	0.40	>.05
Energy	142	7.23	7.21	2.41	1.85	−0.02	.26	0.05	>.05

Table L. Changes in Abilities—Comparisons of Those Who Did and Did Not Reach Middle Management

Variable	Achieved Middle Management (N = 61)		Did Not Achieve Middle Management (N = 106)		N	F Ratio	Significance Level
	Assessment Mean	Reassessment Mean	Assessment Mean	Reassessment Mean			
School and College Ability Test:							
Verbal	46.5	50.4	43.7	48.0	123	0.15	>.05
Quantitative	42.7	43.3	39.4	41.4	123	2.95	>.05
Total	89.3	94.1	83.1	90.0	123	2.36	>.05
Critical Thinking in Social Science	37.9	41.2	35.6	40.0	165	1.37	>.05
Contemporary Affairs	32.5	50.1	29.8	43.0	166	1.42	>.05
In-Basket	2.7	3.1	2.6	2.7	124	1.18	>.05
Business Game	3.5	2.9	3.2	2.7	123	0.26	>.05
Group Discussion (overall)	3.6	2.9	3.0	2.4	123	0.06	>.05

Assessment staff rating on						
Scholastic Aptitude	3.4	3.6	2.9	3.2	167	0.10	>.05
Organizing and Planning	3.2	3.1	2.7	2.6	124	0.01	>.05
Decision Making	2.9	2.9	2.6	2.3	124	2.10	>.05
Creativity	2.9	2.6	2.4	2.2	165	0.00	>.05
Human Relations Skills	3.0	2.8	2.6	2.2	167	0.53	>.05
Behavior Flexibility	3.2	2.8	3.0	2.4	167	1.13	>.05
Likeableness	3.0	2.9	3.0	2.5	69	4.84	<.05
Forcefulness	2.9	3.0	2.7	2.5	164	3.84	<.05
Oral Communications Skills	3.4	3.2	2.9	2.7	167	0.06	>.05
Perception of Threshold Social Cues	3.2	3.3	2.9	2.6	166	4.62	<.05
Assessment factor						
Intellectual abilities	6.3	6.5	5.6	5.9	164	0.36	>.05
Administrative skills	6.1	6.0	5.5	5.2	164	0.60	>.05
Interpersonal skills	9.0	8.3	8.3	7.7	164	0.10	>.05
Management ability rating	3.2	3.4	2.4	2.5	123	0.62	>.05

Table M. Changes in Abilities—Comparisons of Prediction Groups (True Positives, False Positives, False Negatives, True Negatives)

Variable	True Positive (N = 39)		False Positive (N = 22)		False Negative (N = 20)		True Negative (N = 42)		N	F Ratio	Significance Level
	Assessment Mean	Reassessment Mean	Assessment Mean	Reassessment Mean	Assessment Mean	Reassessment Mean	Assessment Mean	Reassessment Mean			
School and College Ability Test:											
Verbal	47.3	50.9	47.5	50.4	44.8	49.5	41.8	46.7	123	1.23	>.05
Quantitative	42.4	43.2	40.2	42.2	43.4	43.3	39.0	41.0	123	1.14	>.05
Total	89.8	94.5	87.7	93.1	88.2	93.2	80.7	88.3	123	1.18	>.05
Critical Thinking in											
Social Science	39.1	41.6	38.4	40.9	35.3	40.1	34.9	39.4	123	2.32	>.05
Contemporary Affairs	39.4	54.2	34.5	51.7	17.2	40.9	23.0	37.8	123	0.78	>.05
In-Basket	2.9	3.1	3.1	3.0	2.1	3.0	2.4	2.5	123	1.64	>.05
Business Game	3.7	3.0	3.8	2.9	3.2	2.7	2.9	2.5	123	1.29	>.05
Group Discussion	3.9	3.0	3.9	2.5	3.0	2.6	2.6	2.3	123	5.70	<.01

Assessment staff rating on										
Scholastic Aptitude	3.6	3.7	3.5	3.4	2.9	3.5	2.7	3.0	123	4.14	<.01
Organizing and Planning	3.5	3.3	3.3	3.0	2.6	2.9	2.5	2.5	123	1.28	>.05
Decision Making	3.3	3.0	3.3	2.8	2.8	2.7	2.3	2.1	123	2.58	>.05
Creativity	3.1	2.7	3.0	2.1	2.4	2.4	2.2	2.0	123	3.18	<.05
Human Relation Skills	3.4	3.0	3.1	2.3	2.4	2.5	2.2	1.9	123	3.71	<.05
Behavior Flexibility	3.6	2.8	3.5	2.5	2.4	2.6	2.5	2.1	123	5.47	<.01
Likeableness	3.3	3.1	3.9	3.0	2.7	2.8	2.8	2.3	69	2.35	>.05
Forcefulness	3.1	3.1	3.5	2.5	2.4	2.7	2.3	2.3	123	6.53	<.01
Oral Communications Skills	3.7	3.2	3.5	2.7	3.0	3.1	2.6	2.5	123	3.04	<.05
Perception of Threshold Social Cues	3.5	3.4	3.5	2.8	2.6	3.0	2.6	2.5	123	4.72	<.01
Assessment factor										
Intellectual abilities	6.9	6.7	6.4	6.3	5.0	6.1	5.1	5.6	123	5.21	<.01
Administrative skills	6.7	6.3	6.6	5.7	4.8	5.5	4.8	4.6	123	2.03	>.05
Interpersonal skills	10.1	8.4	10.0	6.8	6.9	7.6	7.0	6.1	123	9.98	<.01
Management ability rating	3.6	3.5	3.3	2.9	2.5	3.2	2.0	2.2	123	4.70	<.01

Table N. Motivational Changes—Comparisons of Those Who Did and Did Not Reach Middle Management

Variable	Achieved Middle Management (N = 61)		Did Not Achieve Middle Management (N = 106)		N	F Ratio	Significance Level
	Assessment Mean	Reassessment Mean	Assessment Mean	Reassessment Mean			
Assessment factor							
Stability of Performance	6.3	5.7	5.5	5.3	164	1.32	>.05
Work Motivation	6.5	7.0	6.6	6.2	164	1.61	>.05
Career Orientation[1]	2.7	3.0	4.6	4.7	164	0.11	>.05
Dependency	9.4	8.2	10.6	8.7	164	3.04	>.05
Assessment staff rating on							
Tolerance of Uncertainty	3.1	2.7	2.6	2.4	163	1.24	>.05
Resistance to Stress	3.2	3.0	2.8	2.8	162	0.58	>.05
Inner Work Standards	3.3	3.4	3.0	3.0	164	0.69	>.05
Primacy of Work	3.1	3.6	3.0	2.9	165	9.56	<.01
Need Advancement	3.6	3.5	3.0	3.0	167	0.02	>.05
Need Security	3.4	3.3	3.7	3.9	165	2.60	>.05

					N		p
Ability to Delay Gratification	3.1	3.1	3.5	3.3	161	0.92	>.05
Need for Superior Approval	3.5	3.2	3.8	3.3	166	0.76	>.05
Need for Peer Approval	3.0	2.5	3.5	2.9	167	0.02	>.05
Goal Flexibility	2.9	2.6	3.4	2.5	163	4.61	<.05
Self-Objectivity	3.1	3.2	2.9	2.7	166	4.49	<.05
Energy	3.5	3.5	3.1	2.9	166	1.27	>.05
Realism of Expectations	3.2	3.3	3.3	2.9	165	8.20	<.01
Bell System Value Orientation	3.3	3.6	3.3	3.2	165	4.77	<.05
Social Objectivity	2.9	2.9	2.7	2.7	165	0.10	>.05
Interview rating on							
Tolerance of Uncertainty	6.1	6.6	5.4	6.4	84	0.69	>.05
Inner Work Standards	7.6	8.5	7.1	7.5	128	1.37	>.05
Primacy of Work	7.0	7.4	6.2	5.9	135	1.57	>.05
Need Advancement	7.7	7.2	6.6	5.8	149	0.82	>.05
Need Security	6.2	6.5	7.6	7.5	91	0.56	>.05
Ability to Delay Gratification	5.7	6.1	5.9	5.8	127	0.70	>.05
Need for Superior Approval	7.9	5.3	7.8	6.0	112	2.13	>.05
Need for Peer Approval	6.7	5.4	7.4	7.2	41	1.62	>.05

Table N. Motivational Changes—Comparisons of Those Who Did and Did Not Reach Middle Management

Variable	Achieved Middle Management (N = 61)		Did Not Achieve Middle Management (N = 106)		N	F Ratio	Significance Level
	Assessment Mean	Reassessment Mean	Assessment Mean	Reassessment Mean			
Goal Flexibility	5.1	4.5	5.5	4.8	139	0.01	>.05
Energy	7.4	7.8	7.1	6.8	142	2.63	>.05.
Bell System Value Orientation	7.6	7.2	7.3	6.8	138	0.00	>.05
Social Objectivity	6.1	7.2	5.9	6.8	124	0.15	>.05
Projectives ratings on							
Optimism–Pessimism	6.4	7.0	6.2	6.2	167	2.20	>.05
General Adjustment	6.0	6.6	5.8	6.1	167	1.23	>.05
Self-Confidence	5.9	6.6	5.6	5.9	167	1.52	>.05
Affiliation	6.1	5.5	6.4	6.1	167	0.56	>.05
Work or Career Orientation	6.4	7.0	6.1	5.7	167	5.70	<.05
Leadership Role	6.3	6.5	5.8	5.9	167	0.29	>.05

Dependence	5.7	5.8	6.3	6.4	167	0.00	>.05
Subordinate Role	6.0	5.4	6.2	6.0	167	1.14	>.05
Achievement Motivation	6.6	6.8	6.2	5.7	167	2.90	>.05
Rotter Incomplete Sentences Blank	12.2	12.2	12.4	12.4	167	0.00	>.05
Edwards Personal Preference Schedule—need for							
Achievement	18.4	20.5	17.2	19.6	167	0.24	>.05
Deference	12.0	11.1	11.9	11.2	167	0.18	>.05
Order	12.2	11.9	11.8	11.8	166	0.08	>.05
Exhibition	15.3	14.8	15.6	15.4	167	0.32	>.05
Autonomy	12.2	14.4	11.6	13.6	167	0.03	>.05
Affiliation	14.2	11.6	15.1	13.0	167	0.54	>.05
Intraception	15.8	14.5	15.5	15.3	167	2.04	>.05
Succorance	8.1	8.1	9.3	8.2	167	1.93	>.05
Dominance	21.2	21.7	20.3	21.2	167	0.40	>.05
Abasement	10.1	10.2	11.1	9.9	164	2.92	>.05
Nurturance	10.9	10.4	12.0	11.4	167	0.01	>.05
Change	15.7	15.8	16.2	16.7	167	0.36	>.05
Endurance	14.1	14.2	14.8	14.3	167	0.32	>.05
Heterosexuality	16.6	17.3	16.6	16.1	167	1.27	>.05
Aggression	13.3	13.4	11.6	12.6	167	1.44	>.05

Table N. Motivational Changes—Comparisons of Those Who Did and Did Not Reach Middle Management

Variable	Achieved Middle Management (N = 61)		Did Not Achieve Middle Management (N = 106)		N	F Ratio	Significance Level
	Assess-ment Mean	Reassess-ment Mean	Assess-ment Mean	Reassess-ment Mean			
Guilford-Martin Inventory of Factors							
GAMIN							
General Activity	14.1	14.9	13.6	13.7	167	1.07	>.05
Ascendancy	26.6	24.8	26.1	25.7	166	2.66	>.05
Masculinity	25.1	24.3	25.0	26.3	167	8.04	<.01
Self-Confidence	41.2	38.5	39.5	39.3	167	4.94	<.05
Lack of Nervousness	28.8	27.7	29.3	29.9	167	2.56	>.05

[1] A high score on Career Orientation reflects high scores on Need Security and Ability to Delay Gratification and a low score on Need Advancement.

Table O. Motivational Changes—Comparisons of Prediction Groups

Variable	True Positive (N = 39)		False Positive (N = 22)		False Negative (N = 20)		True Negative (N = 42)		N	F Ratio	Significance Level
	Assessment Mean	Reassessment Mean	Assessment Mean	Reassessment Mean	Assessment Mean	Reassessment Mean	Assessment Mean	Reassessment Mean			
Assessment factor Stability of Performance	6.8	5.9	5.9	5.3	5.4	5.2	4.9	4.4	123	0.48	>.05
Work Motivation	7.1	9.2	6.7	6.0	5.3	6.5	5.6	6.4	123	1.61	>.05
Career Orientation[1]	2.5	3.3	3.4	4.6	3.9	4.0	5.0	3.9	110	2.04	>.05
Dependency	9.5	7.9	10.0	9.0	9.3	8.7	10.9	8.7	123	2.28	>.05
Assessment staff rating on Tolerance of Uncertainty	3.3	2.8	2.9	2.6	2.7	2.5	2.4	2.0	123	0.51	>.05
Resistance to Stress	3.5	3.2	3.0	2.7	2.7	2.7	2.5	2.4	123	0.37	>.05
Inner Work Standards	3.6	3.5	3.5	3.0	2.8	3.2	3.0	2.9	123	3.32	<.05
Primacy of Work	3.5	3.7	3.3	3.0	2.6	3.3	2.7	2.7	123	2.31	>.05
Need Advancement	3.8	3.7	3.6	3.0	3.0	3.1	2.7	3.0	123	2.74	<.05
Need Security	3.3	3.2	3.5	3.7	3.8	3.5	4.0	3.9	123	0.59	>.05
Ability to Delay Gratification	3.0	2.9	3.2	3.1	3.4	3.5	3.6	3.3	123	0.54	>.05
Need for Superior Approval	3.5	3.0	3.6	3.2	3.6	3.6	4.0	3.6	123	0.97	>.05

Table O. Motivational Changes—Comparisons of Prediction Groups

Variable	True Positive (N = 39)		False Positive (N = 22)		False Negative (N = 20)		True Negative (N = 42)		N	F Ratio	Significance Level
	Assessment Mean	Reassessment Mean	Assessment Mean	Reassessment Mean	Assessment Mean	Reassessment Mean	Assessment Mean	Reassessment Mean			
Need for Peer Approval	3.1	2.3	3.4	3.1	3.1	2.8	3.5	2.7	123	2.36	$>.05$
Goal Flexibility	2.9	2.6	3.1	2.6	2.7	2.4	3.4	2.4	123	2.04	$>.05$
Self-Objectivity	3.2	3.1	2.8	3.0	3.2	3.2	3.2	3.0	122	0.60	$>.05$
Energy	3.7	3.6	3.6	3.1	3.1	3.4	2.8	2.8	123	3.19	$<.05$
Realism of Expectations	3.6	3.3	3.6	3.7	3.3	3.5	3.3	2.9	121	1.32	$>.05$
Bell System Value Orientation	3.5	3.5	3.5	3.1	3.0	3.7	3.4	3.1	123	4.28	$<.01$
Social Objectivity	3.0	2.9	2.7	2.7	2.7	2.7	2.6	2.4	123	0.16	$>.05$
Interview rating on Tolerance of Uncertainty	6.2	6.4	6.0	5.7	6.1	6.7	5.3	5.8	59	0.28	$>.05$
Inner Work Standards	8.0	8.4	7.1	7.8	7.2	8.5	7.0	7.3	98	1.15	$>.05$
Primacy of Work	7.3	7.4	6.6	6.4	6.7	7.1	6.2	5.4	100	1.17	$>.05$
Need Advancement	8.1	7.4	7.2	5.8	7.1	6.8	6.4	5.9	110	0.82	$>.05$
Need Security	6.0	6.7	6.8	6.9	6.6	6.1	7.8	7.8	64	0.37	$>.05$
Ability to Delay Gratification	5.8	6.0	6.6	6.1	5.5	6.2	6.0	5.5	91	0.63	$>.05$
Need for Superior Approval	7.9	5.3	8.5	6.6	7.9	5.5	8.0	6.1	79	0.50	$>.05$

Need for Peer Approval	6.8	5.2	7.3	7.2	6.7	5.7	7.1	6.2	35	0.29	>.05
Goal Flexibility	1.7	2.0	1.5	3.0	1.4	2.4	2.1	2.6	68	1.06	>.05
Energy	7.6	8.0	9.1	7.1	6.9	7.3	6.6	6.8	105	2.86	<.05
Bell System Value Orientation	8.9	8.2	9.0	5.1	9.8	7.4	8.8	5.3	97	0.28	>.05
Projective ratings on Optimism–Pessimism	6.3	7.0	7.0	6.0	6.5	6.8	6.0	6.1	123	2.45	>.05
General Adjustment	6.0	6.7	6.3	6.2	5.8	6.4	5.5	5.9	123	0.87	>.05
Self-Confidence	6.0	6.8	6.2	5.8	5.3	6.2	5.2	5.8	123	1.76	>.05
Affiliation	6.3	5.3	6.1	5.6	5.9	5.8	6.8	6.0	123	0.63	>.05
Work or Career Orientation	6.7	7.4	6.2	6.0	5.7	6.3	5.9	5.3	123	1.82	>.05
Leadership Role	6.6	7.0	6.4	6.3	5.5	5.7	5.2	5.4	123	0.19	>.05
Dependence	5.6	5.4	5.3	5.5	6.2	6.5	6.8	6.7	123	0.32	>.05
Subordinate Role	5.9	5.1	5.8	5.4	6.4	6.0	6.7	6.3	123	0.36	>.05
Achievement Motivation	6.8	7.0	6.6	6.2	6.1	6.5	5.6	5.1	123	0.85	>.05
Rotter Incomplete Sentences Blank	121	122	125	129	119	122	123	125	123	0.24	>.05
Edwards Personal Preference Schedule— need for											
Achievement	18.4	20.4	18.1	19.7	18.5	20.5	17.1	20.0	123	0.61	>.05
Deference	12.5	11.0	12.0	11.2	11.2	11.2	11.7	12.0	123	2.11	>.05
Order	12.3	12.7	10.4	10.0	12.6	10.7	12.5	12.7	123	1.44	>.05
Exhibition	15.1	14.8	14.9	15.1	16.0	15.1	14.7	15.0	123	0.59	>.05
Autonomy	11.6	14.3	12.6	13.3	12.5	14.5	11.6	14.0	123	0.78	>.05
Affiliation	14.6	10.8	16.5	14.8	13.6	12.5	14.8	11.9	123	2.28	>.05

Table O. Motivational Changes—Comparisons of Prediction Groups

Variable	True Positive (N = 39)		False Positive (N = 22)		False Negative (N = 20)		True Negative (N = 42)		N	F Ratio	Significance Level
	Assessment Mean	Reassessment Mean	Assessment Mean	Reassessment Mean	Assessment Mean	Reassessment Mean	Assessment Mean	Reassessment Mean			
Intraception	16.6	14.8	15.3	15.6	14.0	14.2	15.4	14.7	123	1.59	>.05
Succorance	8.3	7.7	8.2	8.0	8.4	9.5	9.7	8.3	120	1.19	>.05
Dominance	21.8	22.3	20.9	21.8	20.6	21.4	19.7	20.6	123	0.11	>.05
Abasement	9.4	9.8	11.4	10.1	11.2	10.9	11.8	9.4	121	3.66	<.05
Nurturance	10.6	10.0	12.7	11.5	11.2	10.6	11.3	11.0	123	0.15	>.05
Change	15.7	15.6	16.2	18.4	15.8	16.1	16.2	15.9	123	1.60	>.05
Endurance	14.3	14.7	14.4	14.0	13.4	13.5	15.6	15.1	123	0.25	>.05
Heterosexuality	15.8	17.0	15.0	15.7	18.0	17.4	17.0	16.8	123	0.48	>.05
Aggression	12.9	14.1	12.0	11.7	14.0	12.4	11.0	12.6	123	2.67	<.05
Guilford-Martin Inventory of Factors GAMIN											
General Activity	14.9	15.5	14.0	14.4	12.6	13.5	13.4	13.0	123	0.46	>.05
Ascendancy	27.7	25.3	27.8	26.8	25.2	24.5	25.6	25.3	122	0.96	>.05
Masculinity	25.0	24.5	25.0	25.0	25.8	24.5	25.0	26.5	123	1.89	>.05
Self-Confidence	41.4	38.6	38.1	39.0	40.9	38.5	39.1	40.0	123	2.73	<.05
Lack of Nervousness	28.6	27.6	30.4	31.1	29.5	28.1	28.7	30.4	123	1.39	>.05

[1] A high score on Career Orientation reflects high scores on Need Security and Ability to Delay Gratification and a low score on Need Advancement.

Table P. Expectations and Attitudes—Means and Standard Deviations by Year

Date	Total Sample			Achieved Middle Management			Did Not Achieve Middle Management		
	Mean	Standard Deviation	N	Mean	Standard Deviation	N	Mean	Standard Deviation	N
Expectations Assessment									
Assessment	25.98	9.00	167	27.26	9.26	61	25.24	8.80	106
1st year follow-up	20.48	8.91	133	21.02	9.11	56	20.09	8.80	77
2nd year follow-up	17.13	10.02	135	17.96	10.16	57	16.51	9.94	78
3rd year follow-up	14.66	10.02	152	18.05	8.62	60	12.46	10.28	92
4th year follow-up	10.93	11.04	161	14.62	10.71	61	8.67	10.68	100
5th year follow-up	9.43	10.89	163	11.36	10.52	61	8.27	11.00	102
6th year follow-up	9.26	11.03	160	13.03	10.46	59	7.06	10.80	101
7th year follow-up	9.69	10.92	158	16.36	7.55	59	5.72	10.71	99
General Management Attitude									
1st year follow-up	14.51	4.43	128	15.19	4.02	52	14.04	4.65	76
2nd year follow-up	13.20	4.74	132	14.19	4.56	57	12.44	4.77	75
3rd year follow-up	12.83	4.95	150	13.76	4.43	59	12.23	5.20	91
4th year follow-up	12.21	5.08	161	13.92	4.51	61	11.16	5.15	100
5th year follow-up	12.20	5.46	162	13.35	4.88	60	11.52	5.69	102
6th year follow-up	11.75	5.29	161	13.80	4.99	60	10.53	5.10	101
7th year follow-up	11.22	5.01	157	13.44	4.79	59	9.89	4.67	98

Table P. Expectations and Attitudes—Means and Standard Deviations by Year

Date	Total Sample			Achieved Middle Management			Did Not Achieve Middle Management		
	Mean	Standard Deviation	N	Mean	Standard Deviation	N	Mean	Standard Deviation	N
Personal Satisfaction									
1st year follow-up	9.41	3.61	128	9.77	3.19	52	9.16	3.88	76
2nd year follow-up	9.31	3.86	132	9.54	3.52	57	9.13	4.12	75
3rd year follow-up	7.87	3.80	150	8.20	3.87	59	7.65	3.75	91
4th year follow-up	8.58	4.37	161	9.72	4.34	61	7.88	4.26	100
5th year follow-up	9.13	4.27	162	10.13	4.64	60	8.54	3.95	102
6th year follow-up	8.83	4.33	161	10.30	4.22	60	7.96	4.17	101
7th year follow-up	8.42	4.13	157	10.17	4.13	59	7.37	3.77	98
Job Satisfaction									
1st year follow-up	6.55	1.80	128	6.54	1.74	52	6.55	1.85	76
2nd year follow-up	6.14	1.77	132	6.23	1.80	57	6.08	1.75	75
3rd year follow-up	6.69	3.14	150	7.53	3.43	59	6.14	2.83	91
4th year follow-up	5.09	2.14	160	5.69	2.09	61	4.72	2.10	99
5th year follow-up	5.22	2.11	162	5.43	1.99	60	5.10	2.17	102
6th year follow-up	5.06	2.31	161	5.63	2.21	60	4.72	2.31	101
7th year follow-up	4.96	2.13	157	5.68	2.05	59	4.52	2.08	98

Table Q. Attitude Scales—Means and Standard Deviations Through Year 5 for Remainder and Terminator Groups

| Scale | Group | Years after Assessment | | | | | | | | | | | |
| | | 1 | | | 2 | | | 3 | | | 4 | | |
		Mean	S.D.	N	Mean	S.D.	N	Mean	S.D.	N	Mean	S.D.	N
General Management Attitude	Remainder	14.51	4.43	128	13.20	4.74	132	12.83	4.95	150	12.21	5.08	161
	Voluntary	15.60	4.16	25	13.65	4.74	23	13.48	4.03	21	10.94	3.68	16
	Forced	12.41	5.27	32	12.26	5.50	23	11.13	5.08	16	9.08	4.91	12
Attitude toward Supervision	Remainder	13.16	4.59	128	11.47	4.88	131	11.13	5.46	150	10.19	4.97	161
	Voluntary	13.76	4.39	25	12.13	5.27	23	11.95	4.90	21	10.19	4.39	16
	Forced	11.50	4.96	32	10.26	5.59	23	9.56	5.32	16	6.33	4.83	12
Personal Satisfaction	Remainder	9.41	3.61	128	9.31	3.86	132	7.87	3.80	150	8.58	4.37	161
	Voluntary	9.44	4.51	25	9.74	4.78	23	8.48	4.45	21	7.56	4.18	16
	Forced	7.50	4.06	32	6.78	3.36	23	6.88	4.75	16	6.67	2.31	12
Job Satisfaction	Remainder	6.55	1.80	128	6.14	1.77	132	6.69	3.14	150	5.09	2.14	160
	Voluntary	6.32	2.29	25	5.22	2.39	23	4.38	2.80	21	4.25	2.35	16
	Forced	5.28	2.39	32	4.83	2.76	23	5.38	2.73	16	4.25	2.34	12

Table R. Attitude Scales—Comparisons of Remainder and Terminator Groups One Year After Assessment

Scale	Remainder (N = 128) Mean	Standard Deviation	All Terminators (N = 57) Mean	Standard Deviation	Mean Difference	t	Significance Level
General Management Attitude	14.51	4.43	13.81	5.05	0.70	0.95	>.05
Attitude toward Supervision	13.16	4.59	12.49	4.81	0.67	0.90	>.05
Personal Satisfaction	9.41	3.61	8.35	3.33	1.06	1.72	>.05
Job Satisfaction	6.55	1.80	5.74	2.38	0.81	2.55	<.05
			Voluntary Terminators (N = 25)				
General Management Attitude	14.51	4.43	15.60	4.16	−1.09	1.14	>.05
Attitude toward Supervision	13.16	4.59	13.76	4.39	−0.60	0.61	>.05
Personal Satisfaction	9.41	3.61	9.44	4.51	−0.03	0.04	>.05
Job Satisfaction	6.55	1.80	6.32	2.29	0.23	0.55	>.05
			Forced Terminators (N = 32)				
General Management Attitude	14.51	4.43	12.41	5.27	2.10	2.31	<.05
Attitude toward Supervision	13.16	4.59	11.50	4.96	1.66	1.80	>.05
Personal Satisfaction	9.41	3.61	7.50	4.06	1.91	2.60	<.05
Job Satisfaction	6.55	1.80	5.28	2.39	1.27	3.32	<.01

REFERENCES

Bayley, Nancy, "On the Growth of Intelligence," *American Psychologist*, 1955, Vol. 10, pp. 805-818.

Bray, Douglas W. and Donald L. Grant, "The Assessment Center in the Measurement of Potential for Business Management," *Psychological Monographs*, 1966, Vol. 80, No. 17 (whole No. 625).

Bridgman, Donald S., "Success in College and Business," *The Personnel Journal*, Vol. IX, No. 1, June 1930, pp. 1-19.

Campbell, John P., Marvin D. Dunnette, Edward E. Lawler, III, and Karl E. Weick, Jr., *Managerial Behavior, Performance, and Effectiveness*, McGraw-Hill Book Company, New York, 1970.

Gifford, Walter S., "Does Business Want Scholars?" *Harper's Magazine*, May 1928.

Grant, Donald L. and Douglas W. Bray, "Contributions of the Interview to Assessment of Management Potential," *Journal of Applied Psychology*, Vol. 53, No. 1, Part 1, February 1969, pp. 24-34.

Grant, Donald L., Walter Katkovsky, and Douglas W. Bray, "Contributions of Projective Techniques to Assessment of Management Potential," *Journal of Applied Psychology*, Vol. 51, No. 3, June 1967, pp. 226-232.

Kappel, Frederick R., "From the World of College to the World of Work," *Bell Telephone Magazine*, Vol. 41, Spring 1962, pp. 3-16.

Knapp, Robert A. and Joseph J. Greenbaum, *The Younger American Scholar: His Collegiate Origins*, University of Chicago Press, Chicago, 1953.

Murray, Henry A., *Explorations in Personality*, Oxford University Press, New York and London, 1938.

Office of Strategic Services Assessment Staff, *Assessment of Men*, Holt, Rinehart & Winston, New York, 1948.

Rychlak, Joseph F. and Douglas W. Bray, "A Life-Theme Method for Scoring of Interviews in the Longitudinal Study of Young Business Managers," *Pschological Reports*, Monograph Supplement 1-V21, 1967.

White, Robert W., *Lives in Progress*, Holt, Rinehart, and Winston, New York, 1952.

INDEX

Ability, *see* Intellectual ability; Management abilities; and Skills
Achievement, need for, 43-44, 149
Adjustment, 150-151, 178-179
Administrative skills, 78-80, 132-133, 135-142
Advancement, need for, 43-44, 154
see also Career orientation
Assessment center, 6-7, 17-35
Assessment factors, 78-79, 196-200
changes in, 130-154, 178-179, 208
and potential, 78-79
and success, 135-142, 151-154, 188-191
Assessment judgments, basis for, 76-81
of potential, 45-46, 69-70
of termination, 172-173
staff conference, 29-30
Assessment techniques, 17-18, 21, 188-191, 209
Business game, 20-22, 133-134
cognitive tests, 28-29, 41-42
contribution to factors, 78-80, 196-200
Group Discussion Problem, 22-24, 133
In-Basket, 24-26, 79-80, 132-133, 189-190
Interview, 28, 42-43, 144
Leaderless Group Discussion,
22-23, 133
Manufacturing Problem, 20-22, 133
Personality inventories, 144-145
Projective tests, 26-28, 42-43, 144-145
Assessment variables, 18-20
changes in, 145-148, 206-207
and factors, 78-79, 145-149
and potential rating, 76-78
and success, 76-78, 151-154
Attitudes, 154, 157
changes in, 158-163, 227-228
and success, 158-163
and termination, 174-176, 229-230

Bayley, N., 132, 231
Bell System, 56-58
departments, 61-65
recruiting, 4, 10-14
Biographical information, at assessment, 36-37
at reassessment, 66-67
and termination, 171-172
performance in college, 41-42
Bray, D. W., 4, 42, 78, 79, 82, 231
Bridgman, D. S., 12, 231
Business games, *see* Assessment techniques

Campbell, J. P., 3, 231

233

Inventories, expectations, 38, 154-156
personality, 144-154, 210-211

Job assignments, 58-62
and potential, 58-59
and success, 64-66
variety of, 63-66
see also Job challenge
Job challenge, 70-76, 80-81, 155-156, 162, 191-192
and potential, 74-76
and success, 70-76
Job environment, 56-67, 70-71, 179-180
Job involvement, 83-84, 179-180
and success, 97-101, 127-128
Job performance, evaluation of, 59
Job satisfaction, see Satisfaction

Kappel, F. R., 12, 231
Katkovsky, W., 27, 42, 143, 231
Knapp, R. A., 41, 231
Knowledge, of current events, 130-132, 178
technical, 129-130, 178

Leaderless Group Discussion, 22-23, 133
Leadership, see Interpersonal skills and Motivation
Life themes, 82-92
changes in, 93-97, 201
of enlarger-enfolders, 103-114, 180-185
job challenge and, 182
of prediction groups, 102-106, 114-126, 204-205
of success groups, 97-102, 127-128, 202-203

Management abilities, 78-80, 129-130
and success, 135-141
changes in, 130-134, 214-217
overall, 134-135, 141-142
Management development, 2-5, 59-

60, 63, 70-71, 80-81, 130, 141-142, 176-192
Management levels, 57-58
Management potential, 45-46, 76-78
and assessment factors, 78-79
and job challenge, 74-76
and success, 69-74
Management Progress Study, 3-9
design, 6-8, 55
implications of, 80-81, 141-142, 176-192
purpose, 4-5
sample, 3, 6-8
Management progress variables, see Assessment variables
Management success, 64-65
and assessment factors, 135-142, 151-154, 188-191
and assessment variables, 76-78, 151-154
and attitudes, 158-163
and biographical information, 12-13
and expectations, 156-157
and job challenge, 70-76
and job involvement, 97-101, 127-128
and life themes, 97-102, 127-128, 202-203
and opportunity, 64-66, 68-69, 80-81
and personal characteristics, 135-141, 151-154
and potential, 69-70
and satisfaction, 159-161
Manufacturing Problem, 20-22, 132
Mental ability, see Intellectual ability
Mishler, E. G., 38
Mobility, 63-65
Motivation, 42-45, 143-154, 191-192, 218-226
accepting employment, 14-16
achievement, 43-44, 149
advancement, 43-44
and success, 151-154
career orientation, 79-80